P9-DOE-032

OPPOSING
VIEWPOINTS®
SERIES

Dictatorships

DISCARD

Other Books of Related Interest:

At Issue Series

Does the World Hate the United States?

Is Foreign Aid Necessary?

Current Controversies Series

Espionage and Intelligence

Global Viewpoints Series

Civil Liberties

Genocide

Workers' Rights

Introducing Issues with Opposing Viewpoints

The Election Process

Opposing Viewpoints Series

The Arab Spring

Democracy

Human Rights

Libya

DISCARD

"Congress shall make no law ... abridging the freedom of speech, or of the press."

First Amendment to the US Constitution

The basic foundation of our democracy is the First Amendment guarantee of freedom of expression. The Opposing Viewpoints series is dedicated to the concept of this basic freedom and the idea that it is more important to practice it than to enshrine it.

OPPOSING VIEWPOINTS® SERIES

Dictatorships

Tom Lansford, Book Editor

GREENHAVEN PRESS
A part of Gale, Cengage Learning

GALE
CENGAGE Learning·

Detroit • New York • San Francisco • New Haven, Conn • Waterville, Maine • London

GALE
CENGAGE Learning·

Elizabeth Des Chenes, *Director, Publishing Solutions*

© 2013 Greenhaven Press, a part of Gale, Cengage Learning.

Gale and Greenhaven Press are registered trademarks used herein under license.

For more information, contact:
Greenhaven Press
27500 Drake Rd.
Farmington Hills, MI 48331-3535
Or you can visit our Internet site at gale.cengage.com

ALL RIGHTS RESERVED.
No part of this work covered by the copyright herein may be reproduced, transmitted, stored, or used in any form or by any means graphic, electronic, or mechanical, including but not limited to photocopying, recording, scanning, digitizing, taping, Web distribution, information networks, or information storage and retrieval systems, except as permitted under Section 107 or 108 of the 1976 United States Copyright Act, without the prior written permission of the publisher.

For product information and technology assistance, contact us at

Gale Customer Support, 1-800-877-4253
For permission to use material from this text or product, submit all requests online at www.cengage.com/permissions

Further permissions questions can be emailed to permissionrequest@cengage.com

Articles in Greenhaven Press anthologies are often edited for length to meet page requirements. In addition, original titles of these works are changed to clearly present the main thesis and to explicitly indicate the author's opinion. Every effort is made to ensure that Greenhaven Press accurately reflects the original intent of the authors. Every effort has been made to trace the owners of copyrighted material.

Cover Image copyright © Dmitry Nikolaev/Shutterstock.com.

LIBRARY OF CONGRESS CATALOGING-IN-PUBLICATION DATA

Dictatorships / Tom Lansford, book editor.
    pages ; cm -- -- (Opposing viewpoints)
    Includes bibliographical references and index.
    ISBN 978-0-7377-6314-0 (hardcover) -- ISBN 978-0-7377-6315-7 (pbk.)
    1. Dictatorship--Juvenile literature. I. Lansford, Tom.
    JC495.D49 2013
    321.9--dc23
                                                          2013002233

Printed in the United States of America
    1 2 3 4 5   17 16 15 14 13

ACC LIBRARY SERVICES
AUSTIN, TX

Contents

Chapter 3: Are Select Democracies Becoming Dictatorships?

Chapter 4: What Does the Future Hold for Middle Eastern Governments?

Why Consider Opposing Viewpoints?

> *"The only way in which a human being can make some approach to knowing the whole of a subject is by hearing what can be said about it by persons of every variety of opinion and studying all modes in which it can be looked at by every character of mind. No wise man ever acquired his wisdom in any mode but this."*
>
> John Stuart Mill

In our media-intensive culture it is not difficult to find differing opinions. Thousands of newspapers and magazines and dozens of radio and television talk shows resound with differing points of view. The difficulty lies in deciding which opinion to agree with and which "experts" seem the most credible. The more inundated we become with differing opinions and claims, the more essential it is to hone critical reading and thinking skills to evaluate these ideas. Opposing Viewpoints books address this problem directly by presenting stimulating debates that can be used to enhance and teach these skills. The varied opinions contained in each book examine many different aspects of a single issue. While examining these conveniently edited opposing views, readers can develop critical thinking skills such as the ability to compare and contrast authors' credibility, facts, argumentation styles, use of persuasive techniques, and other stylistic tools. In short, the Opposing Viewpoints Series is an ideal way to attain the higher-level thinking and reading skills so essential in a culture of diverse and contradictory opinions.

In addition to providing a tool for critical thinking, Opposing Viewpoints books challenge readers to question their own strongly held opinions and assumptions. Most people form their opinions on the basis of upbringing, peer pressure, and personal, cultural, or professional bias. By reading carefully balanced opposing views, readers must directly confront new ideas as well as the opinions of those with whom they disagree. This is not to argue simplistically that everyone who reads opposing views will—or should—change his or her opinion. Instead, the series enhances readers' understanding of their own views by encouraging confrontation with opposing ideas. Careful examination of others' views can lead to the readers' understanding of the logical inconsistencies in their own opinions, perspective on why they hold an opinion, and the consideration of the possibility that their opinion requires further evaluation.

Evaluating Other Opinions

To ensure that this type of examination occurs, Opposing Viewpoints books present all types of opinions. Prominent spokespeople on different sides of each issue as well as well-known professionals from many disciplines challenge the reader. An additional goal of the series is to provide a forum for other, less known, or even unpopular viewpoints. The opinion of an ordinary person who has had to make the decision to cut off life support from a terminally ill relative, for example, may be just as valuable and provide just as much insight as a medical ethicist's professional opinion. The editors have two additional purposes in including these less known views. One, the editors encourage readers to respect others' opinions—even when not enhanced by professional credibility. It is only by reading or listening to and objectively evaluating others' ideas that one can determine whether they are worthy of consideration. Two, the inclusion of such viewpoints encourages the important critical thinking skill of objectively evaluating an author's credentials and bias. This evaluation will illuminate an author's reasons for taking a particular stance on an issue and will aid in readers' evaluation of the author's ideas.

It is our hope that these books will give readers a deeper understanding of the issues debated and an appreciation of the complexity of even seemingly simple issues when good and honest people disagree. This awareness is particularly important in a democratic society such as ours in which people enter into public debate to determine the common good. Those with whom one disagrees should not be regarded as enemies but rather as people whose views deserve careful examination and may shed light on one's own.

Thomas Jefferson once said that "difference of opinion leads to inquiry, and inquiry to truth." Jefferson, a broadly educated man, argued that "if a nation expects to be ignorant and free . . . it expects what never was and never will be." As individuals and as a nation, it is imperative that we consider the opinions of others and examine them with skill and discernment. The Opposing Viewpoints series is intended to help readers achieve this goal.

David L. Bender and Bruno Leone,
Founders

Introduction

"The transition from tyranny to democracy is very hard. The Syrian people have to handle this in a way that works in Syria. And the brutality of the [President Bashar al-]Assad regime is unacceptable."

—*Jacob Lew,*
US White House chief of staff,
February 12, 2012

Following a month of popular protests, Tunisian dictator Zine El Abidine Ben Ali was driven from power on January 14, 2011. He had ruled his country since 1987. Later, on May 15, US president Barack Obama described the fall of Ben Ali in the following manner: "Hundreds of protesters took to the streets, then thousands. And in the face of batons and sometimes bullets, they refused to go home—day after day, week after week, until a dictator of more than two decades finally left power." Ben Ali's fall prompted a wave of demonstrations and uprisings throughout northern Africa and the Middle East. Dictators who had ruled for decades found their regimes under siege. By the end of the summer, longtime rulers in Egypt, Libya, and Yemen had been overthrown in what became known as the "Arab Spring." Meanwhile, a bloody civil war raged in Syria.

Like other countries in the Middle East, Syria has a history of dictatorship. In 1963 Amin al-Hafiz became leader of Syria in a military coup. He was replaced by Hafez al-Assad in another military uprising seven years later. Assad slowly consolidated power and ruled until his death in 2000. During his leadership, he was reelected president multiple times in rigged elections in which he routinely received more than 90 percent of the vote. Assad brutally suppressed uprisings against his rule in 1971 and 1982. The latter revolt was led by the Islamic group the Muslim Brotherhood and began in the city of Hama. Tens of thousands were killed by the military and security forces who were accused of atrocities against civilians.

Like many dictators, Assad attempted to retain power by exploiting divisions among the Syrian people. Assad belonged to the minority Alawite group that made up about 13 percent of the population. The Alawites are Shiite Muslims, while the majority of Syria's population, approximately 75 percent, is Sunni. Christians make up about 10 percent of the population, and there are significant Druze and Kurdish minorities. Assad rewarded groups such as the Alawites who supported his regime. This created anger and discontent among the majority Sunni groups.

Following Assad's death, his son Bashar al-Assad assumed power. He was elected president in fraudulent voting with 97.2 percent of the vote in 2000, and reelected with 97.6 percent of the vote in 2007. Initially the younger Assad appeared to be a reformer. He released more than six hundred political prisoners after closing one of the country's most notorious political prisons in what was known as the "Damascus Spring." However, repression of dissent continued throughout his tenure, and Assad maintained the state of emergency decree that had been in place since 1963 and that allowed the government to arrest and detain people without warrants.

The Arab Spring motivated Syrian opposition groups to begin to challenge Assad. Beginning on January 26, 2011, protests against the Assad regime were held throughout Syria. The opposition groups wanted an end to the Assad dictatorship. Some protestors sought to create a democracy, others demanded the establishment of a theocratic government such as that in Iran.

The Syrian government responded to the demonstrations with brutal force, arresting thousands. British foreign secretary

William Hague warned the regime that "unless there is mean-ingful change in Syria and an end to the crackdown, President Assad and those around him will find themselves isolated in-ternationally and discredited within Syria." However, new pro-tests in March in Damascus, as well as in the city of Deraa, led to increased violence, including the deaths of dozens of protestors. The United States and other countries placed weap-ons and economic sanctions against the government.

In an attempt to placate the opposition, Assad announced that he would end the state of emergency and release political prisoners. However, police continued to arbitrarily arrest those suspected of opposing the regime. In addition, the army was deployed to stop anti-Assad demonstrations in Damascus and other cities. Nonetheless, pro-democracy demonstrations con-tinued to spread. In June, the army launched an offensive against antigovernment groups in the northern city of Jisr al-Shughour. The fighting killed more than one hundred civil-ians and prompted more than ten thousand Syrians to flee across the border into Turkey.

In response to the brutality of the regime, opposition groups began fighting back. A loose coalition of anti-Assad fighters emerged, calling itself the Free Syrian Army. The group had some successes and attracted defectors from the govern-ment forces. In October, anti-regime factions met in Istanbul, Turkey, to create a united opposition group, the Syrian Na-tional Council. Nonetheless, the opposition remained divided along ethnic and religious lines. Efforts by the United States and western European states to impose stricter sanctions on Syria through the United Nations (UN) were blocked by Rus-sia and China, allies of Assad. The League of Arab States, however, suspended Syria's membership in the group. Assad subsequently agreed to allow league observers into Syria in an effort to develop a peace plan, but the monitors were with-drawn in January 2012 as violence continued to escalate. In August, the UN General Assembly passed a nonbinding resolution that called on Assad to resign. He refused and escalated military efforts to suppress the rebels. By November of 2012, more than forty thousand people had been killed in the fighting, which also created more than 2.5 million refugees.

The case of Syria highlights one of the core differences between dictatorships and democracies. Whereas people can remove unpopular leaders through the ballot box in democratic systems, in dictatorships regime change is often accompanied by violence. For most of human history, dictatorships were the most common form of government, but democracy has increasingly challenged dictatorships. *Opposing Viewpoints: Dictatorships* examines contemporary dictatorships as well as regimes that fell during the Arab Spring in chapters titled Can Dictatorships Be a Good Form of Government?, Are Select Dictatorships Becoming Democracies?, Are Select Democracies Becoming Dictatorships?, and What Does the Future Hold for Middle Eastern Governments? Some of the viewpoints highlight the positive aspects of dictatorships, while others are highly critical of the governmental system. Taken together, the viewpoints help explain why dictatorships continue in an age of growing democracy.

OPPOSING VIEWPOINTS® SERIES

CHAPTER

Can Dictatorships Be a Good Form of Government?

Chapter Preface

Dictatorships are a form of government in which all or most power is concentrated in the hands of an individual or small group. It is an autocratic system in which leaders are not accountable to the people they govern. In other words, dictators rule without the consent of the people.

Dictatorships were the most common form of government for much of human history. Most dictatorships were monarchies in which rulers were titled as princes or princesses, kings or queens, emperors or empresses, sultans, and so forth. In monarchies, power is inherited. Contemporary monarchies include Saudi Arabia, Jordan, and Kuwait, among others. Monarchs often based their legitimacy on religious grounds. For instance, European kings and queens often asserted that their power was based on the divine right of kings—that their power came from a supreme being. In another example, the monarchs of Jordan and Morocco base their legitimacy on the fact that they are descended from the founder of Islam, the Prophet Muhammad.

Often dictatorships are initiated by military figures. A general or other military leader uses the forces under his command to take control of the government. That ruler might then start his own dynasty. For instance, after Henry Tudor defeated other claimants to the English throne, he was crowned Henry VII and started a dynasty that ruled England from 1485 to 1603. Modern dynasties include the Assad family in Syria or the descendants of Kim Il-sung in North Korea.

Dictatorships could also be established through legitimate political processes. For example, in ancient Rome, dictatorial powers would be given to a leader during a time of crisis. In other instances, leaders might legally enter office through elections or other constitutional means but then go on to create an authoritarian regime.

One reason for the durability of dictatorships as a form of government is their efficiency. During times of crisis, a single, charismatic leader might be able to more quickly respond to domestic or foreign threats. Dictators often rise to power by being able to restore order during periods of civil war or other internal conflict. In some cases, dictators have been responsible for significant and positive economic or social transitions.

In the following chapter, journalists, political scientists, and other researchers explore whether a dictatorship can be a good form of government. They explore how dictatorships can either modernize countries or cause them to stagnate. The viewpoints also explore whether dictatorships unify or divide a state, as well as analyze the impact of authoritarian rule on corruption and public life.

"The ruler who moves society to a more advanced stage of development is not only good but also perhaps the most necessary of historical actors."

The Good Autocrat

Robert D. Kaplan

In the following viewpoint, Robert D. Kaplan argues that sometimes dictatorships can be both good and necessary for people if such dictators oversee economic and social transformations that improve the lives of their people. He compares the good and bad characteristics of autocratic rulers in the Middle East and Asia to explain his arguments. Kaplan is an author and senior fellow at the Center for a New American Security. His most recent book is Monsoon: The Indian Ocean and the Future of American Power.

As you read, consider the following questions:

1. According to the viewpoint, what are some examples of dictators who should be overthrown for moral reasons?

2. In Kaplan's view, what ideology is a common basis for benevolent autocracy in Asia?

Robert D. Kaplan, "The Good Autocrat," *The National Interest*, no. 114, July/August 2011, pp. 51–58. Copyright © 2011 by The National Interest. All rights reserved. Reproduced by permission.

3. What is the per capita GDP of Vietnam, as Kaplan reports?

In his extended essay, *On Liberty*, published in 1859, the English philosopher John Stuart Mill famously declares, "That the only purpose for which power can be rightfully exercised over any member of a civilized community, against his will, is to prevent harm to others." Mill's irreducible refutation of tyranny leads him to—I have always felt—one of the most moving passages in literature, in which he extols the moral virtues of Marcus Aurelius, only to register the Roman's supreme flaw. Mill writes:

> If ever any one, possessed of power, had grounds for thinking himself the best and most enlightened among his contemporaries, it was the Emperor Marcus Aurelius. Absolute monarch of the whole civilized world, he preserved through life not only the most unblemished justice, but what was less to be expected from his Stoical breeding, the tenderest heart. The few failings which are attributed to him, were all on the side of indulgence: while his writings, the highest ethical product of the ancient mind, differ scarcely perceptibly, if they differ at all, from the most characteristic teachings of Christ.

And yet, as Mill laments, this "unfettered intellect," this exemplar of humanism by second-century-AD standards, persecuted Christians. As deplorable a state as society was in at the time (wars, internal revolts, cruelty in all its manifestations), Marcus Aurelius assumed that what held it together and kept it from getting worse was the acceptance of the existing divinities, which the adherents of Christianity threatened to dissolve. He simply could not foresee a world knit together by new and better ties. "No Christian," Mill writes, "more firmly believes that Atheism is false, and tends to the dissolution of society, than Marcus Aurelius believed the same things of Christianity."

If even such a ruler as Marcus Aurelius could be so monumentally wrong, then no dictator, it would seem, no matter how benevolent, could ever ultimately be trusted in his judgment. It follows, therefore, that the persecution of an idea or ideals for the sake of the existing order can rarely be justified, since the existing order is itself suspect. And, pace Mill, if we can never know for certain if authority is in the right, even as anarchy must be averted, the only recourse for society is to be able to choose and regularly replace its forever-imperfect leaders.

But there is a catch. As Mill admits earlier in his essay,

> Liberty, as a principle, has no application to any state of things anterior to the time when mankind has become capable of being improved by free and equal discussion. Until then, there is nothing ... but implicit obedience to an Akbar or a Charlemagne, if they are so fortunate as to find one.

Indeed, Mill knows that authority has first to be created before we can go about limiting it. For without authority, however dictatorial, there is a fearful void, as we all know too well from Iraq in 2006 and 2007. In fact, no greater proponent of individual liberty than Isaiah Berlin himself observes in his introduction to *Four Essays on Liberty* that, "Men who live in conditions where there is not sufficient food, warmth, shelter, and the minimum degree of security can scarcely be expected to concern themselves with freedom of contract or of the press." In "Two Concepts of Liberty," Berlin allows that "first things come first: there are situations ... in which boots are superior to the works of Shakespeare, individual freedom is not everyone's primary need." Further complicating matters, Berlin notes that "there is no necessary connection between individual liberty and democratic rule." There might be a despot "who leaves his subjects a wide area of liberty" but cares "little for order, or virtue, or knowledge." Clearly, just as there are good and bad popularly elected leaders, there are good and bad autocrats.

The signal fact of the Arab world at the beginning of this year of democratic revolution was that, for the most part, it encompassed few of these subtleties and apparent contradictions. Middle Eastern societies had long since moved beyond basic needs of food and security to the point where individual freedom could easily be contemplated. After all, over the past half century, Arabs from the Maghreb to the Persian Gulf experienced epochal social, economic, technological and demographic transformation: It was only the politics that lagged behind. And while good autocrats there were, the reigning model was sterile and decadent national security regimes deeply corrupt and with sultanic tendencies. These leaders sought to perpetuate their rule through offspring: sons who had not risen through the military or other bureaucracies, and thus had no legitimacy. Marcus Aurelius was one thing; Tunisia's Zine El Abidine Ben Ali, Egypt's Hosni Mubarak and Syria's Bashar al-Assad, quite another. Certainly, the Arab Spring has proved much: that there is no *otherness* to Arab civilization, that Arabs yearn for universal values just as members of other societies do. But as to difficult questions regarding the evolution of political order and democracy, it has in actuality proved very little. To wit, no good autocrats were overthrown. The regimes that have fallen so far had few saving graces in any larger moral or philosophical sense, and the wonder is how they lasted as long as they did, even as their tumultuous demise was sudden and unexpected.

Yet, the issues about which Mill and Berlin cared so passionately must still be addressed. For in some places in the Arab world, and particularly in Asia, there have been autocrats who can, in fact, be spoken of in the same breath as Marcus Aurelius. So at what point is it right or practical to oust these rulers? It is quite possible to force through political change, which leads, contrary to aims, into a more deeply oppressive, militarized or, perhaps worse, anarchic environment. Indeed, as Berlin intimates, what follows dictatorial rule will not inevitably further the cause of individual liberty and well-being. Absent relentless, large-scale human rights violations, soft landings for nondemocratic regimes are always preferable to hard ones, even if the process takes some time. A moral argument can be made that monsters like Muammar el-Qaddafi in Libya and Kim Jong-il in North Korea should be overthrown any way they can, as fast as we can, regardless of the risk of short-term chaos. But that reasoning quickly loses its appeal when one is dealing with dictators who are less noxious. And even when they are not less noxious, as in the case of Iraq's Saddam Hussein, the moral argument for their removal is still fraught with difficulty since the worse the autocrat, the worse the chaos left in his wake. That is because a bad dictator eviscerates intermediary institutions between the regime at the top and the extended family or tribe at the bottom—professional associations, community organizations, political groups and so on—the very stuff of civil society. The good dictator, by fostering economic growth, among other things, makes society more complex, leading to more civic groupings and to political divisions based on economic interest that are by definition more benign than tribal, ethnic or sectarian divides. A good dictator can be defined as one who makes his own removal less rife with risk.

While the logical conclusion of Mill's essay is to deny the moral right of dictatorship, his admission of the need for obedience to an Akbar or a Charlemagne at primitive levels of social development leaves one facing the larger question: Is transition from autocracy to democracy always virtuous? For there is a vast difference between the rule of even a wise and enlightened individual like the late sixteenth-century Mogul Akbar the Great and a society so free that coercion of the individual by the state only ever occurs to prevent the harm of others. It is such a great disparity that Mill's proposition that persecution to preserve the existing order can never be justified remains theoretical and may never be achieved; even democratic governments must coerce their citizens for a variety of reasons. Nevertheless, the ruler who moves society to a more advanced stage of development is not only good but also perhaps the most necessary of historical actors—to the extent that history is determined by freewill individuals as well as by larger geographical and economic forces. And the good autocrat, I submit, is not a contradiction in terms; rather, he stands at the center of the political questions that continuously morphing political societies face.

Good autocrats there are. For example, in the Middle East, monarchy has found a way over the decades and centuries to engender a political legitimacy of its own, allowing leaders like King Mohammed VI in Morocco, King Abdullah in Jordan and Sultan Qaboos bin Said in Oman to grant their subjects a wide berth of individual liberties without fear of being overthrown. Not only is relative freedom allowed, but extremist politics and ideologies are unnecessary in these countries.

It is only in modernizing dictatorships like Syria and Libya—which in historical and geographical terms are artificial constructions and whose rulers are inherently illegitimate—where brute force and radicalism are required to hold the state together. To be sure, Egypt's Mubarak and Tunisia's Ben Ali neither ran police states on the terrifying scale of Libya's Qaddafi and Syria's Assad nor stifled economic progress with such alacrity. But while Mubarak and Ben Ali left their countries in conditions suitable for the emergence of stable democracy, there is little virtue that can be attached to their rule. The economic liberalizations of recent years were haphazard rather than well planned. Their countries' functioning institutions exist for reasons that go back centuries: Egypt and Tunisia have been states in one form or another since antiquity. Moreover, the now-fallen dictators promoted a venal system of corruption built on personal access to their own ruling circles. And Mubarak, rather than move society forward by dispensing with a pseudomonarchical state, sought to move it backward by installing his son in power. Mubarak and Ben Ali were dull men, enabled by goons in the security services. The real story in the Middle East these past few months, beyond the toppling of these decrepit regimes, is the possible emergence of authentic constitutional monarchies in places like Morocco and Oman.

Both of these countries, which lie at the two geographical extremities of the Arab world, have not been immune to demonstrations. But the protesters in both cases have explicitly called for reform and democracy within the royal system and have supported the leaders themselves. King Mohammed and Sultan Qaboos have moved vigorously to get out in front of popular demands by reforming their systems instead of merely firing their cabinets. Indeed, over the years, they have championed women's rights, the environment, the large-scale building of schools and other progressive causes. Qaboos, in particular, is sort of a Renaissance man who plays the lute and loves Western classical music, and who—at least until the celebrations in 2010 marking forty years of his rule—eschewed a personality cult. The characteristics, then, of the benign dictator are evident, at times hewing to propositions set forth by the likes of Berlin: freedom may come as much from stability as from democracy; leaders must adhere to the will of the people, they need not in all cases be chosen by them. Yet in the Middle East these dictators remain the exception to the rule, and this is why quasi monarchies of the ironfisted Assad or the crazed and tyrannical Qaddafi are now under assault.

The place where benevolent autocracy has struck deep and has systematic roots is Asia. Any discussion of whether and how democracy can be successfully implemented might, because of the current headlines, begin with the Arab world, but the answers such as there are will, nevertheless, ultimately come in from the East. It is in those Asian lands that conventional Western philosophical precepts are challenged.

Real GDP per Capita by Country, 1960–2010

Converted to US dollars using 2010 PPPs (2010 US dollars)

Country	1960	1990	2000	2010
United States	17,368	35,612	44,081	46,844
Canada	14,436	30,040	36,153	39,104
Australia	14,893	27,150	34,101	39,497
Japan	5,938	28,848	31,586	33,612
Republic of Korea	1,510	11,781	20,225	29,184
Singapore	4,331	28,186	42,626	58,240
Norway	14,960	38,474	52,279	55,938
Sweden	13,807	28,668	34,038	39,407

PPPs = purchasing power parities.
Percent changes were calculated using the compound rate method.

TAKEN FROM: *International Comparisons of GDP per Capita and per Hour, 1960–2010*, US Bureau of Labor Statistics, August 15, 2011.

The ideology by which Asian autocrats stand in opposition to the likes of Mill and Berlin falls—to some extent—under the rubric of Confucianism. Confucianism is more a sensibility than a political doctrine. It stresses traditional authority, particularly that of the family, as the sine qua non of political tranquility. The well-being of the community takes precedence over that of the individual. Morality is inseparable from one's social obligation to the kin group and the powers that be. The Western—and particularly the American—tendency is to be suspicious of power and central authority; whereas the Asian tendency is to worry about disorder. Thus, it is in Asia, much more so than in the Middle East, where autocracy can give the Western notion of freedom a good run for its money. The fact that even a chaotic democracy is better than the rule of a Mubarak or a Ben Ali proves nothing. But is a chaotic democracy better than the rule of autocrats who have overseen GDP growth rates of 10 percent annually over the past three decades? It is in places like China, Singapore, Malaysia and Vietnam where good dictators have produced economic miracles. These in turn have led to the creation of wide-ranging personal freedoms, even as these leaders have compelled people against their will on a grand scale. Here the debate gets interesting.

Indeed, probably one of the most morally vexing realizations in the field of international politics is that Deng Xiaoping, by dramatically raising the living standard of hundreds of millions of Chinese in such a comparatively short space of time—which, likewise, led to an unforeseen explosion in personal freedoms across China—was, despite the atrocity of Tiananmen Square that he helped perpetrate, one of the great men of the twentieth century. Deng's successors, though repressive of political rights, have adhered to his grand strategy of seeking natural resources anywhere in the world, wherever they can find them, caring not with which despots they do business, in order to continue to raise the economic status of their own people. These Chinese autocrats govern in a collegial fashion, number many an engineer and technocrat among them, and observe strict retirement ages: This is all a far cry from the king of Saudi Arabia and the deposed leader of Egypt, sleepy octogenarians both, whose skills for creating modern middle-class societies are for the most part nonexistent.

Park Chung-hee, in the 1960s and 1970s, literally built, institutionalized and industrialized the South Korean state. It was Park Chung-hee's benign authoritarianism, as much as the democracy that eventually followed him, that accounts for the political-economic powerhouse that is today's South Korea.

Then, of course, there is the founder of current-day Singapore, Lee Kuan Yew. In 1959, Lee became prime minister of what was then a British colony. He retired from that post over thirty years later (though he continued to exert significant power until very recently). As the British prepared to withdraw in the 1960s, Lee attached Singapore to Malaya, helping to form Malaysia as a bulwark against Indonesian expansionism. When racial tensions between ethnic Malays in the Malay Peninsula and ethnic Chinese in Singapore made the new federation unworkable, Lee seceded and the independent city-state of Singapore was born. When Lee assumed power, Singapore was literally a third-world malarial hellhole beset by ethnic tensions and Communist tendencies; it was barely a country in any psychological sense and it certainly could not defend itself against powerful neighbors. Lee turned it into a first-world technological dynamo and transportation hub, with one of the highest living standards worldwide, and with a military that is among the best anywhere pound for pound. Along the way, a strong national consciousness was forged in the vein of a twenty-first-century trading state. Lee's method of government was not altogether democratic, and his intrusion into people's lives bordered on the petty and anal-retentive: banning spitting, the use of tobacco and chewing gum. The press, of course, was tightly controlled. Whenever criticized, Lee scoffed at how an uninhibited media in India, the Philippines and Thailand had not spared those countries from rampant corruption; multinationals love Singapore in large measure because of its meritocracy and honest government. Yes, Singapore is green with many parks, and so immaculate it borders on the antiseptic. But it is also a controlled society that challenges ideals of the Western philosophers.

For Lee has provided for the well-being of his citizens without really relying on democracy. His example holds out the possibility, heretical to an enlightened Western mind, that democracy may not be the last word in human political development. What he has engineered in Singapore is a hybrid regime: capitalistic it is, but it all occurred—particularly in the early decades—in a quasi-authoritarian setting. Elections are held, but the results are never in doubt. There may be consultations with various political groupings, yet, in fifty years, there is still little sign that the population is fundamentally unhappy with the ruling People's Action Party (though its majority has fallen somewhat). Unsurprisingly, Lee makes liberals supremely uncomfortable. Fundamentally Mill, Berlin and many other Western philosophical theorists and political scientists—from Thomas Paine and John Locke to Francis Fukuyama of late—hold that people will eventually wish to wrest themselves from the shackles of repressive rule. That the innate human desire for free will inevitably engenders discontent with the ruling class from below—something we have seen in abundance in the lands of the Arab Spring. Yet, Confucian-based societies see not oppression in reasonably exercised authority but respect; they see lack of political power not as subjugation but as order. Of course, this is provided we are talking about a Deng or a Lee and not a Pol Pot.

To be sure, Asian autocracies are not summarily successful. Elsewhere, political Confucianism is messier. In Malaysia, Mahathir bin Mohamad lifted his people out of abject poverty and easygoing cronyism to mold another high-tech, first-world miracle; but he lacks virtue because of the tactics he employed as methods of control: vicious campaigns against human rights activists and intimidation of political opponents, which included character assassination. The Vietnamese Communist leadership has lately overseen dynamic economic growth, with, again, the acceleration of personal freedoms, even as corruption and inequalities remain rampant. Think for a moment of Vietnam, a society that has gone from rationing books to enjoying one of the largest rice surpluses in the world in a quarter of a century. It recently graduated in statistical terms to a middle-income country with a per capita GDP of $1,100. Instead of a single personality with his picture on billboards to hate, as has been the case in Egypt, Syria and other Arab countries, there is a faceless triumvirate of leaders—the party chairman, the state president and the prime minister—that has delivered an average of 9 percent growth in GDP annually over the past decade. Nevertheless, Vietnam's rulers remain fearful of public displays of dissatisfaction spread across the Internet. And there is China: Continental in size, it produces vastly different local conditions with which a central authority must grapple. Such grappling puts pressure on a regime to grant more rights to its far-flung subjects; or, that being resisted, to become by degrees more authoritarian. So terrified is its regime of its own version of an Arab Spring that it has gone to absurd lengths to block social media and politically provocative areas of the web.

Here is the dilemma. Yes, a social contract of sorts exists between these citizens and their regimes: In return for impressive economic growth rates, the people agree to forego their desire to replace their leaders. (Truly, East Asian autocracies have not robbed people of their dignity the way Middle Eastern ones have.) But even as such growth rates continue unabated—to say nothing of if they collapse or even slow down—at higher income levels, this social contract may peter out. For as people become middle class, they gain access to global culture and trends, which prompts a desire for political freedoms to go along with their personal ones. This is why authoritarian capitalism may be just a phase rather than a viable alternative to Western democracy.

To be sure, once the basic issues of food and security have been addressed, pace Mill and Berlin, democracy retains a better possibility of getting it right than autocracy. This is because virtuous autocracies are hard to come by and usually rely on the genius of personality; whereas democracy, regardless of the personalities involved, is systemically better positioned to lead citizenries along the path of development. Of course, we will have to wait until China's economic growth slows down, or, failing that, continues until enough Chinese have more access to global culture. Only then can we really begin to draw conclusions about whether democracy represents the final triumph of reason in politics.

The genius of both Rome and America lies ultimately in their institutions, which allowed in the first place for their freedoms. True, the history of Rome—and particularly the death of the Roman Republic—is not in the least uplifting relative to the cause of political expression. But it was Rome's ability to provide a modicum of stability to parts of central Europe and the entire Mediterranean basin—and thus further the cause of personal freedoms (mind you, by the dismal standards of the era)—that is key to its achievement; and something which, in turn, is owed to its imperial superstructure. And as that superstructure became too unwieldy, an emperor like the gruff soldier Diocletian could allow for the division of the empire itself into several administrative parts, thus furthering its life span. America, for its part, is unique in its division of federal, state, and local power over a vast continental landscape, allowing for the full expression of its boisterous democracy. Say what you will about the deficiencies of the United States and particularly those of Rome, but they both indicate a very difficult truth central to the outcome of the Arab Spring: It is not about the expressions of freedom in Tahrir Square so much as it is about the building of legitimate institutions to replace illegitimate ones. And because institutions are hierarchical—and social media like Twitter and Facebook dismantle existing hierarchies—revolutions enabled by new technology do not necessarily lead to the building of governing organizations. Criticism is not enough, someone must wield power; hopefully in a way less coercive than before.

Meanwhile, the Arab Spring has raised the pressure on autocrats the world over to truly be good—or at least better. Though, even if they are, they can never ultimately get it right, as demonstrated by Mill's example of Marcus Aurelius.

> "Joseph Stalin said: 'One death is a trag-
> edy; one million is a statistic.'"

All Dictatorships Are Evil

Sergiu Vidican

In the following viewpoint, Sergiu Vidican examines the psychology of dictators. He argues that there are certain common traits among modern autocrats such as Joseph Stalin and Hosni Mubarak. Vidican also analyzes a series of experiments that examine whether power corrupts even good people or whether bad people naturally seek power and authority. The author also explores why good people often do not act to prevent abuses of power. Vidican is a science journalist for the news group Metrolic and a graduate student at the University of Oradea in Romania.

As you read, consider the following questions:

1. How long did Joseph Stalin rule Russia?

2. According to the viewpoint, what are some common characteristics of dictators?

3. What did a 2010 psychological study reveal about people in high positions with worry-free lives, according to the author?

Sergiu Vidican, "On Dictatorship, Power, and Corruption," Metrolic, February 14, 2011. Copyright © 2011 by Interact Media Group. All rights reserved. Reproduced by permission.

I am certain that you are familiar with the events which took place in Egypt [in early 2011], and with the fact that President Hosni Mubarak finally decided to resign from his position as president.

He was considered by many to be a dictator, as he held on to the power for more than three decades, but he was different than all the other dictators which have ruled over the course of time. It is unknown why he made the choices he made, and why did he want to hold on to the power for such a long period of time. Numerous psychologists and scientists have analyzed him, and they have stated that his reasons might have been different than the reasons of the other dictators. According to the psychologists, he suffered from a certain personality crisis, and as a result he started to see himself as being Egypt, as being the personalization of the country. They believe that he will start to suffer both from a physical and from a psychological point of view in the following weeks, as he will start to realize what has happened. The researchers have stated that the dictators have certain traits in common, and Mubarak has some of these traits. Just like any other dictator, he did not accept the opposition with too much kindness. Just like all the other dictators, he used force and brutality in order to take care of the opposition.

Personality Crises in Power

Joseph Stalin was the ruler of Russia between 1924 and 1953, and he ruled the country with brutality. It has been stated that he killed 3 million people in gulags and through executions, but some say that the numbers are actually higher than that, reaching tens of millions. Many have stated that this sort of behavior is the behavior of an insane person, but there are others who disagree. It has been discovered that Stalin was sane when he committed all those acts. When he was aware of his enemies, he killed only them, but when he did not know who they were, he killed a larger number of people. Of course, a normal person would not do such a thing, but this proves that he made those decisions using logic. He was sadistic, and he was insane, but he made his choices through logical thinking. He did not care about the civilians, all he cared about were his opponents. In order to be able to eliminate them he did what he had to do. His actions are not justified, but this is the way in which he was thinking, the psychologists have stated. Jerrold Post, the director of the political psychology program at George Washington University, said that people such as Stalin suffer from malignant narcissism. These people care only about themselves, about their dreams, they do not care whatsoever about the other people, and they would do anything in order to reach their dream. They would kill, they would torture, and so on.

Mubarak's regime did those things such as torture and killing, but the psychologists have stated that even so, he cannot be compared with Saddam [Hussein], [Adolf] Hitler, or Stalin, who were much tougher and merciless. They often killed people without any reasons, but Mubarak was not like that. The psychologists believe that he had an authority problem, as he simply liked to be in charge, without realizing that he is harming the people. [Post] stated that one of the reasons why Mubarak reacted in the way he did when people started to protest against him was because of his age. He could not comprehend the fact that he was no longer wanted as president, especially since he ruled the country for 30 years. Since he is old, his ruling methods are old as well. He did not realize that the methods he used in the past in order to rule, no longer work nowadays, and that hurts the people. Georgi Derlugian, a sociologist at Northwestern University, who has also analyzed numerous revolutions, has stated that it was very obvious that Mubarak was no longer able to distinguish himself from the country. He considered himself to be the country, and he did not realize that his own well-being is not good for Egypt.

He believes that this is one of the reasons why he attacked the oppression: in order to protect himself, but to protect the country as well. The situation is very interesting, because the oppression wanted to remove him from the power in order to liberate the country from his ruling. They fought for the country, but he believed that they are fighting against it. He was convinced that he was doing his country a favor, there is no doubt about that. One of the most surprising things was the fact that he delivered a very defying speech on 10 of February [2011], only to announce on February 11 that he will resign. He spent so many years at the helm of the country, he has seen lots of changes, and now he has been forced to resign from the position he had. The psychologists have stated that it is very likely that he will wonder about what happened, what he did wrong, and so on. Some said that it is very likely that his health will be affected because of this change. He will feel that he has lost something, but even under these circumstances, the majority of the people have stated that he does not deserve compassion, because he did not show compassion to the people.

The Minds of Dictators

The interesting thing is that the mind works in a very strange manner when it comes to compassion. It has been discovered that when we hear about the death of a person, we get way sadder than when we hear about the death of hundreds of people. Of course, the second scenario is much worse, but we cannot identify with it, so we do not feel the same level of grief as when we hear about the tragic death of an individual. Joseph Stalin said: "One death is a tragedy; one million is a statistic." He might have been right, because the psychologists have stated that this is the exact way in which the human brain sees the killings. Paul Slovic, a researcher at the University of Oregon, said that thanks to the evolution of technology we get to hear about these events as soon as they happen. We

"Mubarak and Farouk as corrupt ex-leaders," cartoon by Chris Grosz, www.Cartoon Stock.com. Copyright © by Chris Grosz. Reproduction rights obtainable from www .CartoonStock.com.

are more informed than ever, yet even so, we do not care too much about what happens in the world. Sure, we are aware of these events, such as the Egypt one, but seeing it in the news does not make us willing to take action. He said that humans react to a single death, but when the number of victims increases, the compassion starts to fade away.

For example, it would not make a difference to us if we would hear that 90 people have died instead of 89. That one extra person would not make a difference because he would have been a part of the bigger picture. Those people simply become a statistic. We would care about those people if we would have lost a loved one, but even so, we would have cared about our loss more than we would have cared about the other 89 people. Slovic said that we as humans have been indifferent to numerous crimes and genocides which have taken place over the course of history. Take the gulags, the Nazi concentration camps, and many other instances in which we were aware of the deaths, but we did nothing in order to stop them. Slovic said that this is the way in which the human mind is formed; this is the way in which we are programmed. In order to test his theory, Slovic showed two different pictures to a group of volunteers. He showed them a picture of six children who were dying, and he told the volunteers that these children would need $300,000 in total in order to be saved. Then he showed them the second picture, with a child who was dying as well, telling them that he needs $300,000 in order to be saved. The interesting thing was that the volunteers were willing to give the money to the single child, even though the same amount of money would have saved all the other six children.

In another study he showed a group of volunteers three different pictures. One showed a starving boy, the other a starving girl and the third one showed them together. The volunteers were less compassionate about the children when they were placed in the same picture. Slovic said that this is quite disturbing, because it shows that the compassion starts to decline even when we are talking about two people instead of one. As I said, these dictators have certain things in common such as narcissism, paranoia, and the lack of compassion. Because of this, the scientists wondered if a regular person could become a dictator, under certain circumstances. The psychologists have stated that a person would be able to become a dictator, but that it would not happen overnight. You see, power has the capacity of corrupting the majority of the people, even if we do not like to admit it. . . . There have been various cases and experiments which have proven this, the most important and famous one being the 1971 Stanford Prison Experiment. During this experiment, a certain number of students were asked to play either the role of the guards or the role of the prisoners. The "prison" was actually the basement of the psychology building of Stanford University. Philip

Zimbardo was the one who conducted the experiment, and he later stated that he did not expect to see these behaviors. The experiment did not last more than a week because of the rough behaviors of the guards. The guards even resorted to torture, whereas the prisoners started to become passive to the abusive treatments, accepted them. On top of that, they even accepted to brutalize the other prisoners in order to be spared from the brutalization. You should keep in mind that these were students, who were not violent and who did not show signs of aggression in the past. It seems that the experiment really managed to bring the evil to the surface. It is said that we all have a certain dark side, which can be brought through certain situations.

Power and the Heart of Darkness

Just think about the novel *Heart of Darkness*, in which a simple man manages to commit lots of awful crimes just to be in command in a certain region. The story might seem a little absurd, but the psychologists have stated that it is very possible for a human being to behave in such a manner in certain conditions. The interesting thing during the Stanford experiment was the fact that Zimbardo himself got affected. He did not see things from the perspective of a psychologist, but from the perspective of a prison guard. He allowed the abuse to take place. This practice is common in prison, or in certain camps, through which the prisoners are encouraged to beat on the other prisoners in order to be spared of certain abuses. People can also be dark in order to protect their own interests. In 2010, a psychological study revealed the fact that people who are in a high position and who have a worry-free life, cannot read the emotions of the other people with too much ease. . . . Because of this, a dictator will not worry too much about the people, as he will not realize that they are feeling bad. Since he cannot see the way in which things really are, he will not try to make a change. The researchers who conducted the study stated that the reason for the lack of understanding is the fact that the one in charge does not make connections with the other people. A dictator will use an iron fist; he will not care about making alliances. On the other hand, the ones who are in a lower position will need to make certain connections and alliances, and thus, they will need to be able to read the people they are dealing with.

When one has the power, he does not need to be empathic towards the other people because he no longer needs those people. On top of that, it was also discovered that the people who have power and authority are more likely to be more impulsive and to make certain ill-founded decisions. The researchers also discovered that the ones who have the power tend to isolate themselves from the other people. In an experiment, the researchers asked the volunteers to draw an "E" on their foreheads. However, prior to doing that, the volunteers were asked to think of themselves as either being weak or powerful. The ones who considered themselves powerful, drew the letter on their foreheads themselves, whereas the weaker ones asked other people to draw the letter. The E made by the powerful ones was backwards. . . . Even if the powerful people had the letter drawn in a wrong manner, they did not care, because since they considered themselves to be powerful, they no longer cared about the opinions of the weaker persons.

The researchers also discovered that when they asked people to consider themselves to be powerful, they were under the assumption that they had control over various things, even in situations which they could not actually control. For example, they believed that they could control the outcome of a dice throw. As you can imagine, the dictators have all these traits, and this is one of the reasons why they end up controlling people in the way in which they do. They no longer feel sympathy for the people, they no longer care about the opinions of the people, and they are under the assumption that they can control everything, even the events over which they have no control. It is a recipe for disaster, or for tyranny, take it as you want it. There are certain psychologists who believe that the power does not actually have the capability of changing a person, but that it offers the people the possibility of putting into practice their beliefs. These researchers have stated that a person does not become evil because of the power, and that only the people who have had those intentions in the first place will become evil. They said that power magnifies the ideas of a person. If he sees himself as being good with more power, he will be good. It is unknown which of these theories is true, but it seems that the majority of the people consider the first one to be valid, that power corrupts people.

> "[Muammar Al Gathafi] transformed the country from one of the world's poorest states into one of the wealthiest (though the wealth was unevenly distributed), with a thriving economy and industry."

Lessons from Libya: Who Defines a Dictator?

Sishuwa Sishuwa

In the following viewpoint, Sishuwa Sishuwa explores the dilemma posed by dictators who improve the lives of their subjects but who rule through tyranny and fear. The author uses the case study of Libya to examine how a dictator was able to dramatically enhance the standard of living of his people. However, the brutality of the regime led to its overthrow. The author also discusses the hypocrisy of the West in its relations with Libya. Sishuwa Sishuwa is a Zambian writer and a Rhodes Scholar at Oxford University in the United Kingdom.

As you read, consider the following questions:

1. When was oil discovered in Libya, according to the viewpoint?

Sishuwa Sishuwa, "Lessons from Libya: Who Defines a Dictator?," *New African*, December 2011, pp. 28–32. Copyright © 2011 by Al Bawaba Ltd. All rights reserved. Reproduced by permission.

2. Which two African dictators have ruled the longest of those Sishuwa mentions?

3. According to the viewpoint, what region armed the rebels who overthrew the Libyan dictator?

The brutal killing of Libyan leader Muammar Al Gathafi at the hands of NATO-supported so-called rebels can only be described as one of the most defining stories of 2011. But with no major outcry coming from Africa and the new Libyan leaders trying to legitimize the killing and make the world believe that the country will be rebuilt from Western inflicted ruins, many questions remain unanswered about the fall of the country. In this opinion piece, Zambian writer Sishuwa Sishuwa probes questions which are on many an African mind. Has Africa learnt anything from the Libyan debacle?

On Monday, 24 December 1951, Libya attained her independence from Italy, the first African country to achieve that feat after the Second World War. A litany of challenges greeted the newly liberated state that, for the next eighteen years, was ruled by a hereditary monarchy under King Idris. These included the backwardness of industry, high incidences of poverty and illiteracy, poor living standards and working conditions for a few who were fortunate to find jobs, and a vast mass of miserable peasants who were in dire need of sufficient land on which to sustain themselves, agriculturally, as most of the arable land was still held by Italian settlers.

These challenges persisted throughout the first two decades of independence, as the fruits of freedom remained elusive for many Libyans, even after the discovery of significant oil reserves in 1959. Their frustrations were worsened by an arrogant, corrupt and intolerant monarchical cabal that presided over considerable underdevelopment, and which tried to disguise the emptiness of its existence behind a magnificent façade of pomp and splendour. Consequently, widespread discontent against the regime mounted. Hugely influenced by the sociopolitical ideological context of the time, including the ideas of then Egyptian president Gamal Abdel Nasser, and inspired by a scarce courage that shows a love of their country, a small band of Libyan patriots, who could not bear the injustices of the regime any longer, rebelled against the monarchy and seized power in a bloodless coup in September 1969.

For the next four decades, Libya's fate was under the reign of the charismatic leader, Muammar Al Gathafi. During that span, he transformed the country from one of the world's poorest states into one of the wealthiest (though the wealth was unevenly distributed), with a thriving economy and industry, accessible state-of-the-art medical facilities, state-funded educational facilities, a working middle class, high standards of living, modern infrastructure, first-class housing, and sufficient water and sanitation. Over the decades he created a genuine welfare state, initiated afforestation of large areas of Libya, and lifted the status of Libya to a middle-income economy. But Al Gathafi's long reign was also marred by extreme authoritarianism, the abolishment of constitutionalism, massive corruption, high levels of intolerance to criticism, forced subservience of the citizens, and frustrations resulting from a lack of participation in the governance of their country and a dangerous absence of open mechanisms through which to air their grievances—deleterious traits which had partly inspired his own rise to power.

Outside Libya, Al Gathafi was both a shining star and a villain. He heavily financed many liberation movements across the continent such as the ANC in South Africa and was widely held as a revolutionary hero in many other African countries. In the West, however, Al Gathafi was intensely regarded as a pariah, who was responsible for the 1988 Lockerbie bombing, who bankrolled rebel movements in countries like Chad, and who, until 2003, invested in weapons of mass destruction, and sponsored terrorism on the continent.

On 20 October 2011, Al Gathafi was captured alive after his convoy was attacked by NATO warplanes and gruesomely killed by the National Transitional Council (NTC) rebels the same day. This was after a protracted rebellion against his rule that began earlier this year.

What lessons can Africa draw from Al Gathafi's life and death?

First there is the fact that there is a limit to which leaders can take the governed for granted. People seek freedom regardless of their standards of living. Freedom means more than having access to social services like education and health, water and sanitation. The Libyan rebellion was not a fight for economic equality but a light for freedom, ethical values, and social justice. Al Gathafi caged his own people for over 40 years and denied them the right to determine how their society should be governed.

Although this is the first rebellion that succeeded in overthrowing Al Gathafi, there were actually more lower-scale agitations accompanying the entire duration of his rule, which showed that people were never tolerant of the violations of their leader, but simply unable to effect the changes they sought to bring into being. His removal from power (not his death) gives inspiration to other troubled Africans on the continent who are struggling against similar injustices—authoritatianism and a lack of full participation in the governance of their countries.

The second lesson is in the form of a question: who is a "dictator" and who defines him or her? Is it the ruled or the "international community", or both? If it is the citizens, is it not their sole preserve and duty to abolish and replace a dictatorial regime? Who arrogates the power to define the other as a dictator? Accordingly, who arrogated the West the power to determine who is a dictator, and who is not, in Africa (and the rest of the world)? Where is the role of African agency in all this?

Isn't it possible that a fundamental policy or ideological differentiation between the West and an African government may lead to the latter's leader being labelled a "dictator"? What happens when both the people of Libya and the West define Al Gathafi as a "dictator", but for different reasons? The people, because of Al Gathafi's ironclad rule and repression, and the West, because it became politically expedient at a certain moment to abandon Al Gathafi as an ally (which he was for most of his reign despite his anti-imperialist overtones), and have him replaced with someone who would serve as a more stable puppet; how do we discern between these contesting definitions in order to avoid having to accept or reject both?

Third, there is the fact that the Libyan question has exposed the vulnerability of Africa in so far as resolving its problems and resisting Western or external interventions. . . . From Cape Town to Cairo, there was a deafening silence while NATO was busy abusing its mandate in Libya and while the deadly sounds of bazookas and AK-47 rifles rang from Benghazi and Tripoli. No African country was heard publicly protesting against the carnage in Libya. The question is why?

When Vladimir Lenin was once asked how he managed to keep control of such a large and vast empire as the Soviet Union, he responded by obtaining a chicken before plucking out all its feathers and letting it go. Unable to determine whether its captor would do more harm to it if it hovered away or protested against the treatment meted out to it, the chicken simply remained still, too traumatised and scared to rebel or do anything. Is Africa in a similar predicament? If so, when will Africa assemble and rebel? If the West was to embark on another colonising mission of the continent, can Africa respond differently to the previous response and emerge victorious? Of course, the question is more complex because there are sharply contrasting interests and desires in every African country and treating a continent of over 54 countries as an undifferentiated monolith is probably wrong. But one may legitimately ask: what would an African victory have looked like in the Libyan case, and would it be a victory for all Africans? However, aren't the challenges that most African countries face similar?

Fourth is the question of what really constitutes good governance and whether or not democracy should be exported. Does good governance consist only of periodic elections and institutional term limits, or rather of improved standards of living, good housing, high literacy and employment levels, among other factors? Or perhaps it presupposes a radically different society based on social and economic relations that call into question all of the human development index indicators we are so used to relying on? When a country's adherence to democratic practices is determined, shouldn't the challenges of democratically ruling a poor and impoverished country—and there are many—be taken into consideration? After the assassination of Al Gathafi, US president Barack Obama said: "We gave him ample opportunity [to transition to democracy], and he wouldn't do it." This raises the question: is it right to force-feed societies that refuse to swallow the pill of democracy at a rapid pace, determined by those who have arrogated themselves the power to feed other societies with their values, without taking into account the unique settings and existing variables of the host society, as we have witnessed in Libya? What really is democracy?

Given the fact that the West has been and continues to be allies with a whole host of non-democracies, isn't a democratic leader or state simply one that remains faithful to Western interests? Is it really the fight for democracy that explains the West's participation in Libya or rather, geopolitics focused on oil revenues and the West's support for Israel is the principal issue at the centre? And since when did the West become a defender of third-world interests without there being anything in it for them? If it was simply the question of Al Gathafi's

No-Fly Zone

6. [The United Nations Security Council] *decides* to establish a ban on all flights in the airspace of the Libyan Arab Jamahiriya in order to help protect civilians;

7. *Decides further* that the ban imposed by paragraph 6 shall not apply to flights whose sole purpose is humanitarian, such as delivering or facilitating the delivery of assistance, including medical supplies, food, humanitarian workers and related assistance, or evacuating foreign nationals from the Libyan Arab Jamahiriya. . . .

8. *Authorizes* member states that have notified the secretary-general and the secretary-general of the League of Arab States, acting nationally or through regional organizations or arrangements, to take all necessary measures to enforce compliance with the ban on flights imposed by paragraph 6 above, as necessary, and *requests* the states concerned in cooperation with the League of Arab States to coordinate closely with the secretary-general on the measures they are taking to implement this ban, including by establishing an appropriate mechanism for implementing the provisions of paragraphs 6 and 7 above.

United Nations Security Council Resolution 1973,
March 17, 2011.

longevity in power, and the desire to install a democratic state that defends human rights, as we are told, why haven't we seen a similar campaign in other countries where we have witnessed widespread human rights violations and leaders who have been in power for as long as the slain Libyan leader?

Surely, aren't Obama and the West aware that Teodoro Obiang Nguema of Equatorial Guinea and José Santos of Angola have both been in power for 32 years, Robert Mugabe in Zimbabwe, 31, Paul Biya of Cameroon, 29, Yoweri Museveni of Uganda, 25, King Mswati III of Swaziland and Blaise Compaoré of Burkina Faso, 24 years? Or is it because geopolitical interests are at play even here and the West is easily pillaging the resources of these countries with the consent of some of these countries' leaderships?

Finally, there is the question of what the death of Al Gathafi says about the current world order and the double standards that characterise it. Doesn't the gruesome assassination of the former Libyan leader violate international law, the very one which the West preaches to others, as established by the Geneva Conventions? Were any lessons really learnt from the Iraq War? Since he was captured alive, why was Al Gathafi not tried? Suggestions that his killing will be investigated and that the West was not aware of it are simply laughable, to say the least. It is the West that armed the rebels who killed Al Gathafi, potentially including those who finally assassinated him. In any case, wasn't the intention of bombing his convoy to kill him in the first place?

Of course, to assign primary responsibility to the West is not to slight the midwifery role or agency of the rebels in Al Gathafi's death. While the latter sold themselves to expedient interests to advance their own greed and grievances, it is the West that provided all the crucial support including ammunition and airplanes in the first place, though significant efforts were made to project an image that the US, at least, was ignorant of Al Gathafi's final capture and death. American President Obama hailed his death as a "momentous day" for Libya. That was expected from him. It is Ban Ki-moon, United Nations secretary-general, who called it a "historic" moment and surprised some of us. Since when did the UN start celebrating the death of its own members? Whose interests was he defending? Yes, Al Gathafi had committed serious atrocities against his own and other people, and his regime, one may add, was increasingly becoming corrupt. But an honest nation or person will always be against any injustice (especially such a violent death as Al Gathafi's was) regardless of the victim, and the worst injustice is to condemn others to the very injustices and crimes which you have projected yourself as fighting against.

However, expecting the West and the current UN to defend human rights, especially those of their perceived adversaries, is probably expecting too much. Hasn't the US been killing "rebels" or "insurgents" and even innocent civilians in rocket bombings in Afghanistan, Iraq, and other parts of the world, under the banner of fighting terrorism, promoting democracy, and without a recourse to justice? Hasn't the UN, especially in recent times, been associated with the most disagreeable of messages and, in the words of Thabo Mbeki, "severely undermined its acceptability as a neutral force in the resolution of internal conflicts"? Mbeki continued: "It will now be difficult for the United Nations to convince Africa and the rest of the developing world that it is not a mere instrument in the hands of the world's major powers. This has confirmed the urgency of the need to restructure the organisation, based on the view that as presently structured the United Nations has no ability to act as a truly democratic representative of its member states."

Like Saddam Hussein, Al Gathafi is no more. Is the world a better place without him? I am simply not persuaded. As opposed to policing others, the West must change its patronising conduct and revisit its relationship with other nations. The current world order, defined by a few countries but imposed on the majority due to the former's political, economic, technological, media, and military might, is unjust, full of hypocrisy and, as Fidel Castro correctly noted in his recent "Reflections" column, "engenders injustice on our planet, squanders its natural resources and is placing humanity's survival at risk". The need to alter and even abolish it is not only a clarion call to action but also an inescapable duty of all third-world countries and those who thirst for justice, if a more humane, secure, and dignified world order is to be created.

> "African dictators distort their econo-
> mies and steal foreign aid as the means
> to buy support from selected segments
> of the populace."

Dictatorships Often Survive with Local Support

Bill Snyder

In the following viewpoint, Bill Snyder argues that dictatorships survive by exploiting ethnic or social divisions within societies. Authoritarian leaders try to bind some groups to the regime through incentives or favoritism, he asserts in this viewpoint. While this buys the loyalty of some, Snyder reasons, these tactics exacerbate differences and create resentment among other groups. The author uses examples from Africa to examine the impact of ethnic favoritism on countries and their governments. Snyder is a San Francisco journalist and frequent contributor to media outlets including the website InfoWorld and the publication BusinessWeek.

As you read, consider the following questions:

1. What term is used to describe regimes that openly steal from their populations, as Snyder reports?

Copyright © 2007 by the Board of Trustees of the Leland Stanford Junior University. All rights reserved. Used with permission from the Stanford University Graduate School of Business. Story by Bill Snyder. "Dictatorships Often Survive with Local Support." Research, "The Control of Politicians in Divided Societies: The Politics of Fear," by Gerard Padro i Miquel, NBER Working Paper 12573, October 2006.

2. Why does Snyder assert that dictatorships usually can maintain excessive public payrolls?

3. According to the viewpoint, what groups benefit most in dictatorships?

All dictatorships are cruel and wasteful. They deprive the populace of basic rights while enriching a small minority at the expense of rational development.

Some maintain power through terror and the naked use of force applied by huge standing armies and police forces. Paradoxically though, many dictatorships survive with the support of a significant swath of the populace. In sub-Saharan Africa, for example, rulers such as Kenya's former president Daniel arap Moi maintain power by exploiting ethnic and regional differences via a policy of selective economic rewards and privileges.

In effect, the deep ethnic divisions found in much of Africa are life insurance policies for dictators.

Ethnic Divisions

African dictators not only deprive their subjects of human rights, they loot their countries so openly that they have become known as "kleptocracies." Efforts by the developed world to aid these economies are often sabotaged by corrupt bureaucracies that siphon off a huge percentage of external development money. Uganda, for example, at one point derived roughly 20 percent of its budget from foreign aid, without noticeable benefits to the population at large.

In a groundbreaking study, Gerard Padro i Miquel, lecturer at the London School of Economics, demonstrated that African dictators distort their economies and steal foreign aid as the means to buy support from selected segments of the populace. He is a former faculty member at the Stanford Graduate School of Business.

Most academic work on dictatorships has focused on the use of violence and repression. But Padro argues that leaders of countries with sharply defined ethnic differences, such as Kenya, could probably not stay in power without the support of their own ethnic group. Although dictators like Moi may not be terribly popular, given the corrupt and repressive nature of their regimes, members of their ethnic group fear that a new leader from a different ethnic group would be much worse for them. "The fear of falling under an equally inefficient and venal ruler that favors another group is enough to discipline supporters," Padro says.

"If they [members of the dictator's ethnic group] decide to oust him, they face a chaotic succession process in which they cannot guarantee the next leader will belong to their group." Thus the dictator can exploit his own people with little fear that they will move to depose him.

Even so, members of the dictator's group do receive certain privileges, often in the form of patronage or public works projects. This is one reason why countries run by dictatorships often labor under the weight of a bloated public payroll and why so many development projects never succeed.

"The use of public money in the form of bureaucratic posts, infrastructure or even access to schools as a form of patronage, as well as the ethnic bias in the allocation of these goods, has been widely documented in Africa. The Gikuyus and later Kalenjin groups in Kenya, northern groups in both Nigeria and Uganda, or Tutsis in Burundi are just salient examples that have reproduced across the continent," says Padro.

Privileges handed out to favored groups must be paid for, of course. You might think that a dictator would settle the bill by taxing the out-of-power ethnic group and not his own. In fact, says Padro, the cost of supporting a dictatorship generally leads to across-the-board tax increases, since the dictator's group has gotten something for its money and won't protest, and the other ethnic groups have no choice in the matter.

This strategy allows the dictator to extract a maximum amount of money from the whole country while spending money on just one group.

Not surprisingly, taxes, both direct and indirect, are levied unevenly and used as a tool to placate supporters. Uneven spending damages the economy since the government chooses which sectors to aid on the basis of political favoritism, not sound policy. "In Ghana and Uganda, among other examples, the coalition that supported the leader extracted resources from the coffee and cocoa planters—both crops that involve substantial specific long-term investment. On the contrary, in Kenya the Gikuyu controlled the coffee-growing parts of the country, and hence the discrimination against these crops was much less evident," writes Padro.

The Benefits of Ethnic Favoritism

It's worth noting, though, that the actual benefits of ethnic favoritism are not spread evenly. Although Padro does not use the word class (he prefers the terms elites and non-elites), it's clear that the wealthy and upper-class members of the dominant ethnic group receive so many privileges that part of the money to pay for them is extracted from the pockets of the poor and working-class members of the same group.

Padro says the methodology of "The Politics of Fear" is fairly standard; he built a mathematical model based on a wide reading of case studies and other secondary sources. But because of the continued instability in East Africa it was not possible to visit at the time he was conducting his research. He points out that mathematical models in the social sciences test ideas for logical consistency, but do not necessarily prove the truth of a particular conclusion. Moreover, few dictatorships keep accurate records of illicit revenue and expenditures.

[Interestingly, the government of Peru did keep detailed records of bribes to politicians, an error that was instrumental in bringing down the government of Alberto Fujimori.]...

Colonialism and Ethnic Favoritism

Over the course of European occupation in Rwanda, elitism was successfully refashioned into racism. By preventing Hutu access to higher education and administrative jobs, they were essentially closed off from the political arena and representation in such. Moreover, the documentation of 'ethnic groups' enhanced the importance of these rigid classifications. No longer was there flexibility between groups. Ethnic boundaries were clearly defined. So Hutu, excommunicated from power, experienced the solidarity of the oppressed. Over time this rift, this pronounced separateness between Hutu and Tutsi, blossomed into hatred. Why? Because of the Europeans who came to colonize and bring the wealth of Western knowledge, but instead brought racist ideologies. Though the roots of this ethnic hatred and in turn ethnic genocide can be tied to European colonialism that does not mean that Europeans can be blamed for these atrocities. According to UN staff members, "the whole world failed Rwanda. . . ."

Troy Riemer,
"How Colonialism Affected the Rwandan Genocide,"
Yahoo! Voices, June 30, 2010.
http://voices.yahoo.com/the-rwandan-genocide-6298766
.html?cat=75. Copyright © 2010 by Troy Riemer.
All rights reserved. Reproduced by permission.

For those who think that democracy would solve the problems of ethnically based dictatorship, Padro has this somewhat discouraging conclusion: "Finally, note that no difference is made between democracy and dictatorship in the model. The evidence from Africa shows that democracies have not behaved differently than dictatorships when supporting kleptocracies and corruption."

Periodical and Internet Sources Bibliography

The following articles have been selected to supplement the diverse views presented in this chapter.

Fouad Ajami	"Demise of the Dictators," *Newsweek*, February 6, 2011.
Ronald Bailey	"The Political Economy of Ending Tyranny," *Reason*, June 2011.
Akua Djanie	"What Are We Really Celebrating?," *New African*, February 2010.
Natasha M. Ezrow and Erica Frantz	"Inside the Authoritarian State: State Institutions and the Survival of Dictatorships," *Journal of International Affairs*, vol. 65, no. 1, Fall/Winter 2011.
John Feffer	"The Twilight of Tyranny?," *Huffington Post*, March 1, 2011.
Linda Frum	"The Real Trouble at Rights and Democracy," *Maclean's*, March 22, 2010.
Futurist	"Futuring the Revolution," May/June 2011.
Jeffrey Goldberg	"Danger: Falling Tyrants," *Atlantic*, June 2011.
Leon Hadar	"Don't Party Like It's 1989," *American Conservative*, April 14, 2011.
Debora MacKenzie	"How to Predict When a Dictatorship Is Ready to Fall," *New Scientist*, March 5, 2011.

OPPOSING
VIEWPOINTS®
SERIES

CHAPTER 2

Are Select Dictatorships Becoming Democracies?

Chapter Preface

From the eighteenth century onward, more and more countries transitioned from dictatorships to democracies. The American Revolution beginning in 1775 led to the creation of a new form of government, a constitutional democracy, and prompted efforts in France and Latin America to end dictatorial rule. Unlike dictatorships, in democracies, governments rule with the consent of the people, and leaders are chosen by the people.

It was not until the end of World War II in 1945 and the subsequent period of decolonization that large numbers of states transitioned to democracy. Even during this period of democratization, some states established new dictatorships. During the Cold War, the Soviet Union supported the creation of authoritarian regimes around the world. Meanwhile, the United States nominally backed democracy but also provided economic and military support to dictatorships that opposed the Soviet Union and its allies.

Among the states that were allied with the Soviet Union were North Korea and Cuba. Following the end of World War II, in 1948 Korea was divided into Communist-controlled North Korea and South Korea, which was supported by the United States. North Korea's Kim Il-sung founded a repressive, authoritarian regime. Although they established dynasties, Communist rulers such as Kim rejected the title of king or emperor. Instead, he was initially called the supreme leader and in 1972 adopted the title president. Kim ruled the country until his death in 1994, when he was succeeded by his son, Kim Jong-il, who ruled until his death in 2011. He was followed by his son, Kim Jong-un.

In Cuba, Fidel Castro led a revolution that overthrew the US-backed dictator Fulgencio Batista in 1959. Castro also assumed dictatorial powers and aligned Cuba with the Soviet

Union. He ruled Cuba until ill health led him to appoint his brother Raúl to succeed him in 2011. Meanwhile, in Myanmar, the former British colony of Burma, a coup in 1962 overthrew the democratic government and initiated a military dictatorship that ruled until 2011.

With the end of the Cold War in 1989, many dictatorships transitioned to democracy. For instance, Communist states in Eastern Europe, such as the Czech Republic, Hungary, and Poland, became fully democratic states. Other countries that had been divided between a Communist half and a non-Communist half, such as East and West Germany, were reunited as democratic states. However, Cuba, North Korea, and Myanmar remained dictatorships.

The following chapter explores the possibility that these three countries might transition to democracies. Myanmar has made the most progress with relatively free elections in 2011, but the military continues to hold significant power. Cuba has enacted some economic reforms but continues to suppress opposition groups. North Korea remains one of the most repressive dictatorships in the world.

> *"The government also loosened restrictions on the media and the Internet, suspended construction of a controversial hydroelectric dam supported by China, and released more than 200 political prisoners."*

Myanmar Has Begun to Democratize

Pauline H. Baker

In the following viewpoint, Pauline H. Baker examines Myanmar's steps toward democracy along with similar efforts in other countries. She highlights the role that political parties play in democratic transitions and explores the many challenges, such as civil war and mass atrocities, faced by newly democratizing states. Ultimately, Baker contends that democracy must be a slow and steady process, otherwise the forces of tyranny will reassert themselves. Baker is a political scientist who is President Emeritus of the nonprofit educational research organization the Fund for Peace.

As you read, consider the following questions:

1. Who was the first woman elected head of state in Africa?

Pauline H. Baker, "The Dilemma of Democratization in Fragile States," *UN Chronicle*, no. 4, December 2011. Copyright © 2011 by United Nations Publications. All rights reserved. Reproduced by permission.

2. According to the viewpoint, what are the main threats to democratizing states?

3. Does the author believe that former warlords should be allowed to campaign for office in states transitioning to democracy?

Conventional thinking juxtaposes democracy and dictatorship as mutually exclusive systems. It is often assumed that when one system collapses, it is replaced by the other, as if this was the natural order of things. Some theorists, such as Francis Fukuyama, argued that liberal democracy had decisively defeated tyranny with the collapse of the Soviet Union, which marked the "end of history". Indeed, since then, while there have been setbacks in countries such as Ukraine and Zimbabwe, dictatorship has been in retreat.

The most dramatic wave of change has been the Arab Spring [referring to a series of demonstrations, protests, and wars across the Arab world that began in late 2010], in which strongmen in North Africa and the Middle East have been deposed since January 2011. In less dramatic fashion, several countries in sub-Saharan Africa have also moved incrementally toward democratic rule over the last decade. According to the *Economist*, since 1991, 30 parties or leaders in sub-Saharan Africa have been removed by voters. While outcomes have varied, and violence has sometimes followed, grassroots political action, not military rule or assassinations, is emerging as the primary method of removing unpopular leaders.

However, states often go through fleeting periods of democratic reform which may not fully materialize, or teeter in the balance for prolonged periods of time. Myanmar [also known as Burma] is an example of democracy crushed for half a century. The military has ruled since 1962, and the current junta since 1988, when it violently suppressed a pro-democracy movement. In 2011, a civilian government was installed, dominated by the same military or ex-military leaders. It initiated a series of positive steps, including giving more freedom to Daw Aung San Suu Kyi, the popular opposition leader who won the 1990 elections. The government also loosened restrictions on the media and the Internet, suspended construction of a controversial hydroelectric dam supported by China, and released more than 200 political prisoners. While these steps are encouraging, Myanmar has far to go. It remains one of the most repressive and closed countries in the world, where the army continues the repression of ethnic minorities, the main opposition political party was banned until November 2011 organization, and hundreds more political prisoners languish in jail, though the government released some prisoners in October 2011.

Nigeria is an example of a country with democratic promise that remains unfulfilled. Credible elections were conducted in 2011, the first since the return of civilian rule in 1999, and it resulted in the historic installation of a president from a minority ethnic group. Yet this singular event, which deservedly earned worldwide praise, did not fundamentally change the political system. While there is a vibrant press, an increasingly active civil society and an enterprising population, the country faces formidable problems, including ethnic, religious, and economic friction; endemic corruption; severe economic inequality; deepening violence; and a political culture dominated by competing cliques of ex-generals and business tycoons who act as behind-the-scenes power brokers. Thus, while Myanmar remains an authoritarian state with inklings of political reform, Nigeria is an electoral democracy with undemocratic traits. In neither country is democratization assured.

Mixed Outcomes

In 1989, there was widespread hope for democratic transformation when the Berlin Wall came down. However, the death knell for authoritarianism had not rung in many of the capitals of the successor republics that followed the collapse of the Soviet Union, especially in central Asia. In Russia, a popular leader with a KGB [Soviet national security agency] background appealed to his people's desire for order and national pride over the chaos of a criminal oligarchy and the loss of superpower status. The result was "managed democracy", which cloaked authoritarian rule in democratic trappings.

Mixed outcomes are also possible in the Middle Eastern countries embroiled in the Arab Spring and in African states struggling with democratization. Most lack the historical experience, institutional foundations, and social consensus to undergo smooth transitions. There are no preordained outcomes. The leadership, time frame, resources, and circumstances are different in each transition. Positive results have been seen, for example, in Liberia, despite two civil wars that killed an estimated 250,000 people. President Ellen Johnson Sirleaf, the first elected female African head of state, who was awarded the Nobel Peace Prize in 2011, succeeded in preventing a recurrence of fighting, getting international debt relief, attracting economic aid, and keeping her country on track toward democracy since she was first elected in 2005. Despite that, Liberia remains a fragile state.

Elections are an essential part of democratization, but they can also be conflict inducing if they are held too soon, are blatantly manipulated, lack transparency, or are marred by violence. Moreover, even if conducted efficiently, they may result in power shifts that not only marginalize powerful elites, but entire communities, creating sectarian or ethnic conflict. The Kenyan elections in 2007 did both.

In Nigeria, northerners did not feel that the 2011 elections were free and fair, as most observers reported. The north—the poorest region in the country—is where most of the post-election violence which killed hundreds was concentrated, and where, perhaps not coincidentally, terrorist incidents attributed to Boko Haram, a radical Islamist movement, have escalated since the polling.

Populations may be loath to return to old authoritarian rulers, but they also do not want to see continued violence. Thus, after a full-blown conflict or revolutionary change, they often turn to new strongmen as saviours to impose order on chaos—often based on clan, ethnic, or religious identities. There is also a temptation to grasp for quick solutions, hold snap elections, push through slap-dash constitutional arrangements, use shotgun power-sharing agreements, or defer to transitional councils led by security forces—measures that undermine the foundation for democracy.

State Building in Transition

In truth, the biggest danger facing fragile states in transition is not the rise of a new dictatorship, as is often assumed, or even the emergence of extremist factions, which usually represent a minority of the population. These outcomes are possible, but the larger threats are civil war, state collapse, mass atrocities, humanitarian emergencies, and a possible breakup of the country.

One way to avoid such scenarios is to institute an intermediate process of state building, focusing not only on writing a new constitution, holding elections, and providing for basic freedoms, but also on building or restructuring core state institutions: the police, military, civil service, and judiciary, legislative and executive branches of government. State building cannot be bypassed by political accommodation. There still needs to be a solid state infrastructure for long-term stability, the provision of public services, adherence to the rule of law, and promotion of economic opportunity.

Thus far, Tunisia has provided the best model of how it should be done. Within a year of driving its former authoritarian leader into exile, Tunisia became the first Arab Spring

Restrictions and Fraud in Myanmar's 2012 Elections

Besides their apparent attempts to block NLD [National League for Democracy] rallies, it has been alleged that local government officials and the USDP [Union Solidarity and Development Party] are intimidating and threatening voters to support the USDP as part of what opposition groups see as a larger "dirty tricks" campaign. Civil servants in the capital of Nay Pyi Taw (Naypyidaw) were reportedly told not to attend NLD rallies. The residents of one village were told they would not be connected to the electric grid if someone in their household attended an NLD rally. Factory workers have reportedly been warned that they will lose their jobs if they do not vote for the USDP. One report alleges that the USDP has a secret election strategy paper calling for the use of bribery, vote buying, intimidation, and fraud to win the parliamentary seats in the by-election.

The NLD has also reported other forms of campaign irregularities. It claims that the official voter registration lists include a significant number of dead people but omit many eligible voters. In addition, the NLD report that in some parts of the country, advance ballots were being collected well ahead of the official dates of March 30 and 31. It was alleged that advanced ballots were used by the ... USDP to steal some of the seats in the November 2010 parliamentary elections.

Michael F. Martin,
"Burma's April Parliamentary By-Elections,"
Congressional Research Service, March 28, 2012.

country to hold elections for a constituent assembly to write a new constitution and appoint an interim government. The gradual and ordered political transition will allow time for the people to shape the structure of government, and for new political formations to emerge, including political parties and civil society. Most of all, it affords the interim government the chance to lay out a road map for the future, including how to structure the transfer of power and set up state institutions. South Africa followed a similar path during its four-year-long transition to a post-apartheid society, from the time that anti-apartheid parties were legalized and political prisoners released in 1990, until the landmark election of Nelson Mandela in 1994. That interim period was crucial for laying the foundation for a peaceful and lasting democratic transition. It was remarkable that there was no external military intervention nor, contrary to widespread expectations, a race war, a collapse of the state, or a return to political violence.

The Role of Political Parties

Democratization in fragile states is a complex process that cannot be rushed nor taken for granted. All parties should be cognizant of certain realities. First, there is no such thing as an instant democracy. No assumptions should be made about the capacity of fragile states to fulfill their democratic aspirations, nor should their capacity to do so be underestimated. What is important is that, whatever the capacity of the newly formed state to transform itself, the process will not occur overnight.

This leads to the second reality—vacillation, even backsliding, are not uncommon. Most states in democratic transition are embarking upon huge tasks—the rebuilding of the state, restoring national cohesion, and creating a representative government. As long as the general trend is in the right direction, one can expect setbacks along the way. Volatility—not stability—is the natural order of things in the march to democracy.

Third, there must be political inclusion with all major factions allowed to present their views for open political discussion, debate, and political participation. However, a minority of spoilers can be destructive. Thus, in fragile states undergoing rapid change, groups or individuals that openly advocate violence, use hate speech, maintain their own militias, or engage in illegal practices should be restricted from running for public office and held accountable under the law so they do not ignite a new wave of retribution or revenge. If former warlords and power brokers want to move from the battlefield to the ballot box, they should be allowed to do so, provided they give up their arms and refrain from keeping private armies in reserve in case they lose elections. Here the international community can be of vital assistance by providing technical support for the disarmament, demobilization, and reintegration of former combatants; supplying legal aid to institute the rule of law; offering financial assistance to get the economy going; and training professionals to run state institutions honestly and efficiently.

Fourth, the conditions must be right for holding elections—a secure and safe environment which allows for a proper nomination process, unrestricted media coverage, full and open campaigning by candidates, and citizen participation without intimidation. There must be electoral transparency, independent monitoring, and a well-trained election staff overseen by a commission of respected individuals, with sufficient authority and financial resources to meet the logistical challenges of nationwide voting, which often takes place over several days, in remote areas, and under extreme weather conditions. While it may sound contradictory, elections are not only an all-important pivotal milestone in a democratic transition, but merely the first step. The real tests will come in the second and third elections, and those that come after, when power is transferred peacefully from one party to another.

The Balancing Act

Beji Caid [el] Sebsi, the 84-year-old transitional prime minister of Tunisia, faced a series of protests after the overthrow of the ousted dictator, Zine El Abidine Ben Ali, with Tunisians demanding jobs, wages, and immediate retribution against the former rulers. It was not always clear that the transition would be a smooth one. [El] Sebsi summarized the dilemma that he and other leaders across the Middle East and Africa are facing today: "Sometimes the proponents of freedom have demands that go beyond logic, and it is more difficult to protect freedom from the proponents of freedom themselves, than from the enemies", he said. "When someone is hungry asking for food, you only give him what he needs", [el] Sebsi noted, describing his step-by-step approach. "You don't give him more, or else he might die".

The collapse of tyranny, [el] Sebsi seems to be saying, is not the end of history: It is just the beginning. Democracy mismanaged, or descending too quickly, could kill nascent freedom, while democracy delayed, or descending too slowly, might lead to a new dictatorship or inspire further insurrection.

> *"Elections of some sort, even by carefully selected elites, or their promise even over grossly extended periods, seem to have become required even by authoritarian, single-party regimes."*

Despite Elections, Myanmar Remains a Dictatorship

David I. Steinberg

In the following viewpoint, David I. Steinberg asserts that the 2010 elections in Myanmar do not represent a shift from military rule to democracy. Instead, he argues that the balloting was actually a way for the military to enhance the legitimacy of its rule in the country and to placate ethnic minorities opposed to the junta. Although some opposition figures were elected to the new parliament, the military continues to dominate the nation's government. Steinberg is Distinguished Professor of Asian Studies at Georgetown University.

As you read, consider the following questions:

1. What percentage of seats in Myanmar's national legislature are reserved for the military?

"Myanmar in 2010: The Elections Year and Beyond," by David I. Steinberg, first appeared in *Southeast Asian Affairs 2011*, edited by Daljit Singh (2011), pp. 173–177. Reproduced here with the kind permission of the publisher, Institute of Southeast Asian Studies, Singapore, http://bookshop.iseas.edu.sb.

2. According to the viewpoint, what is the first stage in establishing a functioning democracy?

3. Which political party won the most seats in the 2010 elections in Myanmar?

The 7 November 2010 elections [in Myanmar, also known as Burma] may have determined the composition of the new government, but they did not change, and specifically were not intended to change, the distribution of effective power, which still rests with the Tatmadaw (armed forces), and is likely to do so into the indefinite future. The State Peace and Development Council (SPDC) efforts—ineffectual at best—to assuage the minorities are unlikely to succeed for several reasons. The minorities have wanted some form of federal system, and many groups have formulated draft constitutions (illegally under Myanmar law and thus they were forced to do so outside the country) for their seven constituent states that incorporated elements of some such preferred system. To the military, however, federalism has been anathema since [general and dictator] Ne Win declared it so in 1962. He considered it the first step toward secession, against which the military has always fought since independence. The government's Border Guard Force concept has exacerbated tensions; it would result in the effective castration of the cease-fire military of key ethnic groups, and thus has been resisted. It is a subject with which the new government in 2011 will have to deal, and there are fears it may try to do so through military force. The 25 per cent active-duty military in the bicameral national legislative, and even in local ones, prompt questions from the minorities that their rights will not be adequately protected. The glass ceiling has meant top positions in the military itself have been denied to both ethnic and religious minorities under this government. The rights stipulated in the constitution for furthering minority cultures, as in the two previous constitutions, are as likely to be ignored as they have been in the past. And censorship, marginally relaxed during the period before the elections, still prevails. The Tatmadaw's filtering of the muddy waters of the new well of a "discipline-flourishing democracy", as Senior General Than Shwe has said in March 2009, is likely to take quite some time.

What Makes a Democracy?

The basic question is not, as much of the media has announced, the issue of democracy and how democratic the new government might be. Adjectivally modified terms such as "discipline-flourishing democracy" are inherently suspect. The more germane issue is: how much is pluralism really built into the new administrative governmental configuration and how much pluralism will the new government allow? The first stage towards any functioning democracy is the diminution of centralized authority—the bane of the Burmese administration for half a century. Critical in this configuration is the role of the minorities, their ability to articulate their views legally, practice their languages and cultures, and develop locally through access to state-controlled resources.

More than any other single problem, minority issues are perennial; they have intensely affected the state since independence in 1948, although foreign observers have concentrated their attention on political and human rights problems. The SPDC, the ruling military junta that is to disappear when a new government is formed in early 2011, but in part will be reincarnated into civilized form, may have believed that by granting minorities more local autonomy, in contrast to national power, than heretofore, they would assuage their fears and aspirations. They were mistaken. As nationalism has grown among the majority Burmans, so has nationalism expanded among the various minorities, of which there are a large, significant, and vocal number. Ethnic identity has become reified, and mythic ethnic as well as Burman and minority histories have been rewritten to solidify modern political and social needs. The country is neither a "nation-state" with a single national cultural identity corresponding to its administrative boundaries, nor is it a "state-nation" with sets of multiple and accepted ethnic/linguistic identities within an overarching, positive national identity.

One question that is continuously asked by knowledgeable observers is: why has the Tatmadaw, as represented by the SLORC/SPDC [formerly the State Law and Order Restoration Council], held the elections in any case? There are likely to be multiple reasons. Their overt power internally was stronger than it has been since the coup of 1988 that brought that new military regime into control. They might have ruled for an indefinite period. The question is important, but the same might have been asked of the militarily controlled 1974 elections that led to the formation of the military-led, single-party socialist authoritarian mobilization system under the Burma Socialist Programme Party (BSPP), also after the passage of a new constitution. The military ruled by decree from 1962 until 1974, and from 1988 to 2011. In both cases, the military has chosen to ensure their civilianized rule through a designated, subservient party.

Elections Have Initiated Some Minority Representation

Elections of some sort, even by carefully selected elites, or their promise even over grossly extended periods, seem to have become required even by authoritarian, single-party regimes (e.g., North Korea, China, etc.), no matter how much they may be manipulated. This may stem from attempts to secure both popular internal and external legitimacy, attempts that may result in Myanmar in questionable successes in either instance. Self-legitimation may have been a motivating force to affect either internal or external audiences, but either may have been beyond the grasp of the Tatmadaw at this

Regime Restrictions in the 2010 Elections

The new election laws [in Myanmar, also known as Burma] were developed by the military government and effectively prohibit long-standing opponents of the regime—political prisoners and any persons wishing to associate with political prisoners—from competing in the polls. The new national election commission lacks independence; the SPDC [State Peace and Development Council] directly appointed its members with no public input.

One of the new laws, on political party registration, has resulted in the silencing of many of the most prominent opposition voices. It required political parties to register or reregister in order to remain in existence and compete in the elections. But they could do so only if none of their members were currently imprisoned based on a court conviction. This requirement presented parties with a choice of either expelling prominent imprisoned leaders or declining to reregister. Under those circumstances, leading opposition groups including the NLD [National League for Democracy], chose not to reregister and were required to shut down and disband.

*"Burma's 2010 Electoral Framework:
Fundamentally Undemocratic—A Legal
and Human Rights Analysis,"*
National Democratic Institute, August 2010.

time. The elections have been unsatisfactory to many in the country; they have been called a "sham" by many Western observers, an assessment subject to some debate, however deeply flawed they obviously have been. Yet the voting was significant, for this was the first time since the elections of 1960 that it will seat some, albeit limited, number of opposition politicians. What public voice they may have is yet to be determined. Even these flawed elections may also have mitigated the intense political frustration that seems to have been evident in much of the society. Internal disturbances seem unlikely at the core of Burman society, if not in the ethnic periphery. It is evident that the Burmese leadership has regarded the results of the election as a great success. Superficially, from their vantage point this is true as it produced the required—demanded—results. But over the longer term severe problems remain.

If, as seems obvious, internal Burma/Myanmar motivation in 1974 and 2010 may have been broadly similar—continued military control—the emphases have been markedly different. Little attention was paid to minority status in 1974, as a seeming myriad of ethnic rebellions and some calls for independence from central (Burman) control were evident. The result was a monolithic centralized administration. In 2010, however, with seventeen official cease-fires with minority groups, the emphasis has not only been ensuring the military's leadership in the society, which in any event has been encased in the constitution of 2008 that is to come into effect with the 2011 new government, but also that the minority sentiments are (partly) assuaged, at least as seen myopically through Burman Tatmadaw eyes. This has been attempted through formation of a national bicameral Hluttaw (legislature), as in the 1947 constitution that lasted until the military coup of 1962, that has specific minority representation, but more importantly through a set of "provincial" legislatures—seven "regional" ones in Burman areas and seven minority "state" legislatures in those parts of the country. How much these may satisfy minority concerns over Burman discrimination and domination are questionable. Such legislatures in minority areas are unique; the first time that such representation has been allowed at local levels in Burmese history. Some elected groups have expressed concerns of fostering their own languages and cultures, as allowed by provisions built into all Burmese constitutions but heretofore neglected. Each of these legislatures at all levels will have 25 per cent representation by active-duty military chosen by the minister of defence, who (according to the constitution) must be a military officer. Thus, assuaging the minorities has been tempered by a strong military hand.

Election Results

The sweep by the Union Solidarity and Development Party (USDP), together with the mandated 25 per cent active-duty military seats, was ubiquitous at the national Hluttaw level: 77 per cent of the seats (128) in the Upper House and 79 per cent (257) it the Lower House. Of the total of 1,157 seats contested, the USDP won 875. At the "provincial" level (that is, at the regional and state Hluttaw level), however, the situation is less cohesive. The USDP won all the Burman areas with between 61 and 73 per cent of the seats, which when added to the 25 per cent military, gives them complete command. In the minority areas, however, with the exception of the Kayah State which was completely swept by the USDP, the USDP won only between 30 to 46 per cent of the seats. With the addition of the military seats, of course, control still rests with the state's designated actors. Whether pro-government and opposition members of the same nationality will feel that ethnic solidarity trumps politics on local issues is now an important but unanswerable question, and one that may evolve over time. Members of all legislatures are officially subject to constraints on freedom of speech related to national unity, security, and other desiderata, all of which are also mandated in the constitution.

Legislative control over minority regions does not automatically translate into a political or military paramount position. To ensure control over minority areas, the state must in some manner deal with the minority armies, which in the case of the Wa and Kachin groups are significant and compounded by their presence on the China border. Minority military leadership not only fear Burman control, they also fear contestations from their own peoples. The junta's Border Guard Force plan, under which each cease-fire battalion would be integrated into the army (as the constitution requires that there be only one Tatmadaw) and have approximately 10 per cent regular army and one-third of battalion leadership, have been resisted by the major cease-fire groups—the Wa, Kachin, Mon, and others, and almost two years of deadlines to agree to that plan have been missed. The last deadline of 1 September 2010 stipulated that if the plan were not accepted, the cease-fires would be considered void. The result has been the government's rejection of elections in certain areas controlled by the minority groups, and growing tensions before the elections were held. The new government of 2011, led by the military both in and out of uniform, will have to deal with this dissatisfaction, even potential unrest and a possible reversion to armed conflict in certain areas. Heightened tension is evident in the region and there have been suggestions of a minority pact that if one group is attacked, all will respond. As observers have noted: "But based on the new political system, it seems inevitable that the post-2010 political arrangement should give greater voice to ethnic communities on issues of local governance, something that has been largely absent in the past. This dynamic, if it develops over time, is very different from the centralized, hierarchical governance of ethnic areas that has characterized Burma's post-independence period. . . . The election has not diffused Burma's state of conflict."

> "Today, living in an economy that is still in shambles, North Koreans typically have three choices: scurry for goods on the black market, starve, or flee the country."

Watching *Titanic* in Pyongyang

Geoffrey Cain

In the following viewpoint, the author reports on Witness to Transformation: Refugee Insights into North Korea, *by Stephan Haggard and Marcus Noland. This report on the views of refugees from North Korea suggests that this dictatorship is on the verge of collapse. After suffering through famine, inflation, black market trading, and a disastrous attempt at currency manipulation, many people try to flee the country. Fleeing to China often results in being returned to North Korea where individuals face torture, imprisonment, or worse. The refugees' stories reveal black market subversion of official policy, open protest on occasion, and determination to escape from the harsh conditions. Geoffrey Cain covers North and South Korea for* Time *magazine.*

Geoffrey Cain, "Watching *Titanic* in Pyongyang," *The Washington Monthly*, July/August 2011. Copyright © 2011 by The Washington Monthly. All rights reserved. Reproduced by permission.

As you read, consider the following questions:

1. According to the viewpoint, when did the founding father of North Korea die?

2. How many people does the author estimate died in North Korea in the mid-1990s from mass starvation?

3. According to the author, what was the effect of the monetary reform of 2009?

What the first systematic survey of North Korean refugees tells us about life inside the Hermit Kingdom, and about whether the regime might be ready to fall.

Witness to Transformation: Refugee Insights into North Korea, *by Stephan Haggard and Marcus Noland, Peterson Institute for International Economics, 256 pp.*

Ever since the founding father of North Korea, Kim Il Sung, unexpectedly died of a heart attack in 1994, pundits and policy makers have announced the same news every year: the collapse of the world's most repressive and recondite government is imminent. In the middle of a famine in 1997, for instance, a CIA panel concluded that the regime of Kim Jong Il would fall within five years. Seven years later, near the Chinese border, an explosion ripped through a train station Jong Il had traveled through just eight hours earlier. Some Korea watchers proclaimed that the blast was an assassination attempt, and a precursor to insurrection. The explosion, it turned out, was caused by a chemical leak.

Even though the world's most militarized country has not yet disintegrated, analysts were prudent to warn that the conditions for sudden ruin were in place. In the past two decades, North Koreans have struggled through famine, floods, political prison camps, and a slipshod currency reform. Now they're faced with an increasingly volatile Kim Jong Il, who, while in poor health, is attempting to prove to North Koreans that his youngest son, Kim Jong Un, will be the country's next strong and unifying leader. Today, living in an economy that is still in shambles, North Koreans typically have three choices: scurry for goods on the black market, starve, or flee the country.

By most conservative estimates, more than 100,000 North Koreans have chosen the last option, making the perilous trek across the Chinese border and sometimes into Thailand, Vietnam, and Mongolia, where they attempt to enter the safety of South Korean consulates. The lucky ones start new lives south of the border. Their less fortunate compatriots, many of whom wander around China unable to set down roots, are sent home by Chinese police to face torture, imprisonment, and worse.

These exiles may just be the world's best resource for understanding what is happening in North Korea. In their recent book, *Witness to Transformation: Refugee Insights into North Korea*, political economists Stephan Haggard and Marcus Noland present the first-ever methodical study of public opinion among North Korean refugees. For a field in which most studies are limited to anecdotes, interviews, and oral histories, the statistics in *Witness to Transformation* are refreshingly precise—and they affirm much of what the West has always suspected about the Hermit Kingdom.

Haggard and Noland drew on a survey pool of 1,700 defectors who lived in China and South Korea from 2004 to 2008. The refugees' assessments of the North Korean regime are fervently negative: nearly all refugees living in China, for example, cited poor economic conditions as the reason for leaving North Korea, while a third of those who settled in South Korea pointed to political discontent as their motive for leaving. Haggard and Noland's study divides recent North Korean history into four waves of economic change, and categorizes the refugees by the periods during which they left the country.

The first of these periods began in the early 1990s with the dissolution of the Soviet Union. North Korea, hugely dependent on its Communist patron, was deprived of the food and fuel subsidies that had, until then, artificially propped up its economy. By the mid-1990s, the country was gripped by a horrific famine. North Korea's fraying socialist-state food distribution system was unable to handle the task of getting food to the entire populace. Mass starvation claimed between 600,000 and a million lives, in a country of twenty-one million people. North Koreans responded to the famine by bartering their possessions on the black market. Everything was fair game, and everyone who could, took part—from ordinary folks selling off household goods to officials selling off natural resources, weapons, and drugs. Foreign governments donated food aid, hoping to feed at least a third of the population, but half the respondents in Haggard and Noland's survey said they were unaware of foreign food aid before they left North Korea. Among those who did know about the aid, more than three-quarters reported not receiving it.

During the second economic wave—what the authors call the post-famine period of 1999 to 2002—the authorities introduced reforms to accommodate the black market. They increased food prices to ease food providers off government subsidies and encourage production, and they raised wages. But the new policies set off uncontrollable inflation of 100 percent per year, prompting the party to eventually revert to socialist programs.

This led to the third wave, known as the retrenchment period, from 2003 to 2005. Officials brought back the government's food distribution system, banning all private trade in grain. They also threatened to expel foreign donor aid groups. Even so, 70 percent of Haggard and Noland's respondents said they made most of their meager earnings through private trading. The post-retrenchment period followed in 2006 and beyond, a time when tougher socialist restraints in tandem with poor harvests and global price increases once again set off inflation. They also led to the worst food shortages since the famine of the mid-'90s. In late 2009, the government introduced a surprise monetary reform: they knocked two zeroes off the currency and, in an attempt to cripple informal traders, limited the number of old bills that North Koreans could trade in at about $40. The move effectively erased most people's savings. Protests ensued—enough to prompt the regime to issue an unprecedented public apology.

The currency reform could be considered a culmination of a rocky two decades, but the North Korean power clique hasn't budged. Still, refugees who formerly held military and police posts swear the regime can't hold out much longer if its information apparatus falls apart. "Do you actually think we believed what the government told us?" one former North Korean police commander told me in his office in Seoul, the South Korean capital. "Of course not. We got together after work and watched bootleg copies of *Titanic* and *Superman Returns*. We always knew life on the other side was better, but we stayed quiet. We didn't know what anyone else thought."

In a military state that has a virtual lock on the flow of information and a vast security apparatus, this refugee's discretion is what the report's authors call "preference falsification," or the tendency of people to keep their adverse beliefs secret because they don't know about others' allegiances. But there's evidence that the information barriers are being knocked down. Haggard and Noland found that an increasing number of refugees were watching foreign news reports, especially during the retrenchment period—and that this act was associated with negative views of the regime.

Despite the insights they gleaned, Haggard and Noland note that the interviews come with one caveat: that these refugees are not perfectly representative of the attitudes of the entire population because they are potentially its most disaffected sample. Still, the research follows a long academic tradition of gathering information from refugees who escaped from formerly closed states, such as China and the Soviet Union.

The authors partially got around the representation problem through statistical modeling. They created projections of the views of the general population based on the refugees' characteristics—age, gender, and occupation, as well as life experiences such as receipt of food aid or arrest and detention—offering a remarkable glimpse into the closed state.

Since the famine in the 1990s, humanitarian do-gooders and policy makers have tried unsuccessfully to alleviate the plight of North Koreans even as they hope to persuade Kim Jong Il to give up his nuclear weapons and join the community of nations. Their attempts have included engagement known as the "Sunshine Policy," six-party talks, and the donor aid of the late '90s. More importantly, however, the world needs to push China to change its refugee policy. China has a policy of repatriating North Korean defectors because it recognizes them as "economic migrants" and therefore not refugees under the 1951 United Nations Refugee Convention, to which China is a signatory. But China's assertion rests on an inconsistency. One legal basis for claiming refugee status is a fear of persecution upon return to the fatherland—a stipulation that should make refugees out of nearly all North Korean defectors. Still, North Korea and China remain stubbornly impervious to blandishments and change.

What, then, might lead to a collapse of North Korea? Andrei Lankov, a prolific historian of the country, told me that three factors will be needed for revolt: a way for the dissidents to communicate with each other and with the outside world, a reasonable alternative to the current government, and a chance that the revolt will succeed. A better government is certainly possible for a country at rock bottom, and a chance for victory may be there. As this year's North Africa protests have shown us, an angry populace can topple strongmen with little forewarning.

The third aspect of communication seems to be gaining a hold, an assertion backed by the data in *Witness to Transfor-*

mation. The protests against the currency reform in 2009 were scant and disorganized, but they revealed that the government was willing to reverse policies when it faced opposition. Giving more reason for concern, North Korea appears to be experiencing yet another food shortage—an embarrassment after it asked charities and foreign governments, including famine-struck Zimbabwe, for assistance last spring. The recipe for discontent is brewing, and even if the regime does not lose its hold on power, some North Koreans will continue to subvert Kim Jong Il's agenda in simpler, quieter ways.

> *"Alas for its beleaguered citizens, North Korea is set for a whole lot more misery now that the successors seem to have stabilized their positions."*

North Korea's Dictatorship Will Endure

John Fraser

John Fraser offers a pessimistic view, in the viewpoint that follows, of the future of North Korea. Fraser highlights the brutality of the current regime. He also analyzes the historic and contemporary ties between North Korea and China. Fraser contends that while the current regime may not survive much longer, it is likely to be replaced by another authoritarian government, one that is similar to the current Chinese system. Fraser is a Canadian journalist who chaired the Canadian Journalism Foundation and is the chair of the board for Massey College.

As you read, consider the following questions:

1. What titles has Kim Jong-un adopted, according to Fraser?

John Fraser, "From Mao to Now: Pyongyang's Funerary Pomp and Underlying Terror Mirror the Darkest Days of Its Communist Neighbour," *Maclean's*, January 16, 2012. Reproduced by permission.

2. How large is North Korea's military and active reserve forces, as Fraser reports?

3. Upon what model did Kim Il-sung base North Korea's political system?

Nightmares are best left un-revisited, but the death on Dec. 17 [2011] of the "Dear and Great Leader" of North Korea, Kim Jong-il, deserves a deeper look down a particularly grisly memory lane. The entire [spectacle] of the death and succession to the third generation Kim Jong-un, already dubbed "Respected" and "Supreme Commander," evokes some of the worst propaganda excesses of the Maoist regime in Communist China, especially during the Great Proletarian Cultural Revolution, nearly half a century ago.

The pictures of North Koreans amassed in central squares across the country, sobbing their grief to the nation and the world, are almost identical to the pictures that came out of China in 1976 when the Great Helmsman [of the People's Republic of China, Mao Zedong] reluctantly gave up the ghost. Militarized mass mourning is at the heart of these wretched regimes, as if the forced or brainwashed operatic bawling of the masses can—through sheer volume if nothing else—comfort the worried dinosaurs who struggle to maintain the totalitarian status quo.

When people ask what it was like in China during the Hundred Flowers Campaign (1955–57), or Great Leap Forward (1958–60), or the Cultural Revolution itself (1966–68), you just have to say: "Tune in to North Korea." Ditto for forced labour camps, human rights abuses, avoidable starvation, and all sorts of mind-numbing terror campaigns to engender "enthusiasm" in the masses—a cowed and brutalized population ignored by a world that can't do much about their lot except call their regime "evil."

North Korea and China

It is also a regime unsurprisingly protected by the People's Republic of China, which largely props the country up in bad times and worse times for its own self-interests. Alas for its beleaguered citizens, North Korea is set for a whole lot more misery now that the successors seem to have stabilized their positions. Two current world-beating records guarantee this: the worst human rights abuses of any nation on earth; and this is combined with the most militarized society anywhere (more than one million in uniformed service and another 6.3 million in active reserve forces, in a population of barely 24 million).

The cruelly comical nature of the regime has long been established, even before Kim Jong-il (Kim the Second) was a featured puppet character in the 2004 American satirical film *Team America*. Kim the Second's father, Kim Il-sung (Kim the First), was the original nightmare who defined the character of North Korea and actually modelled his "revolution" on China's brutal Maoist regime. For "Mao Zedong Thought," Kim the First offered the concept of "Juche"—an ideological mumbo jumbo in which mankind is the master-genius of all action and the justification for the fully loaded totalitarian state, now being passed along to his grandson.

Passed along, but—with luck and the forces of history—not necessarily for some future Kim the Fourth. The misery North Koreans must still endure will last for however long it will take before the regime either collapses from the inside thanks to its own inadequacies, excesses and corruption (like the Soviet Union and East Germany), or its people rise up in righteous and bloody rage (like Albania or Romania). A third possibility exists, of course, which is the one the world largely hopes will happen, and that is the China model, for want of a better phrase. The China model will see a limited amount of internal turmoil a few years after the bloated Kim heir fizzles in the wake of competing factions within the North Korean military. Probably, a "sensible and visionary" military leader will take over and guide the county into a China-like compromise in which sedate authoritarianism and unredeemed capitalism discover, as they did in China, that they can be kissing cousins.

Lessons from China

For the moment, though, leave aside the Communist world's extraordinary version of royal succession ("The Brutal Monster is dead, long live the Brutal Monster"). Ponder instead the lessons learned from China, which one day will be discovered about the North Korean regime. Using what the world has learned about the final period of state Maoism in China (which includes the period immediately following his death, when the party and state were under the nominal leadership of chairman Hua Guofeng—now confined to what chairman Mao himself delighted to refer to as "the dung heap of history"), we know for sure:

- That there are thousands of Korean political prisoners, some of whom will survive and tell their tales. There will be stories of both extraordinary bravery and craven cowardice. Wait for it.

- That the economic absurdities of the regime will eventually make it implode, but probably not before another period of mass starvation caused by bad planning, bad leadership and world-class corruption. Wait for it.

- That traditional religions are thriving underground and will resurface with a vengeance the moment there is any relenting by the regime or after its eventual downfall. Wait for it.

- That regime conflicts and disagreements, almost wholly shrouded from the public, are raging even as we as-

The Layers to Ruling
North Korea Today

Ruling North Korea today is far more complex than it was during the country's last leadership transition in 1994, upon the death of Kim Jong-il's father, the country's founder and "Great Leader" Kim Il-sung. Two decades of chronic food shortages—which peaked in the famine of the late 1990s that killed between 5%–10% of the country's approximately 22 million people—have caused the breakdown of the state-run distribution system and the emergence of official and clandestine markets, as ordinary North Koreans have had to fend for themselves to feed their families. More North Koreans are exposed to the outside world than ever before. Some venture back and forth into China, own cell phones, have access to foreign radio and television broadcasts, and are able to purchase foreign products. The police state has become highly corruptible, and access to foreign exchange has become a new path to power and protection. The "Great Successor," as Kim Jong-un has been dubbed by the official North Korean media, has had little time to gain experience managing various personal and group interests that have proliferated among the North Korean elite. Many North Korea experts will be watching for signs that these groups and individuals—including one or both of Kim Jong-un's older brothers—are maneuvering to assert themselves and their interests.

Mark E. Manyin, "Kim Jong-il's Death:
Implications for North Korea's Stability and U.S. Policy,"
Congressional Research Service, January 11, 2012.

sume everything is settling down for the reign of Kim the Third. This includes internal struggles within the hierarchy of the all-powerful armed forces. Wait for it.

- That the younger generation of the elite—the children of state and military leaders—will be the motor force behind change, but not before some of them will be branded traitors and subjected to "rigour" as examples to scare the others. They will be executed in public stadiums before crowds of over 100,000. Wait for it.

And what will North Korea be like when the walls of totalitarianism come tumbling down? It could be a lot like the China of today, with Korean cultural embellishments, or—if the North is really lucky like East Germany has been really lucky—as part of thriving, bustling, freedom-loving South Korea. When it will happen or how it will happen is, obviously, impossible to predict, but the fact that it will happen is a no-brainer. That, at least, must supply a few nightmares for all the entourage around Kim the Third who, if North Koreans are lucky, will also go down in history as Kim the Last.

*"Young Cubans are starting to publicly
demand that the regime make tangible
improvements in their lives."*

Fidel's Children

Joseph Contreras

In the following viewpoint, Joseph Contreras examines the impact that youth have on efforts to democratize and reform Cuba. The author contends that Cuba's youth are far more inclined to protest against government oppression than were their parents. He also argues that Cuban leaders are starting to acknowledge the problems within their system, as large numbers of Cuban citizens continue to flee the country for the United States. Contreras is a journalist and author whose works include In the Shadow of the Giant: The Americanization of Modern Mexico.

As you read, consider the following questions:

1. How many Cubans are estimated to have fled to the United States in the two-year period before September 2007?

2. How many signatures does Contreras assert students gathered for a petition for greater freedom at their university?

Joseph Contreras, "Fidel's Children," *Newsweek*, vol. 151, no. 9, March 3, 2008. Copyright © 2008 by Newsweek. All rights reserved. Reproduced by permission.

3. What Cuban blog is mentioned in the viewpoint as being especially critical of the government?

Cuba's leader has resigned, and the nation's youth are starting to push back.

For years, Fidel Castro has been a living anachronism. A stalwart Communist in an age of free markets and democracy, he ruled a Cuba largely cut off from a world prospering through international trade. By the end he was out of touch at home as well, both metaphorically and literally. For 19 months, the ailing 81-year-old leader had stayed out of sight, too sick to venture out, reduced to publishing ponderous "reflections" on the front page of the Cuban Communist Party's organ, *Granma*. By the time he resigned last week, there was something almost anticlimactic about it. Cubans—including émigrés in Miami and elsewhere—have waited so long for a change they barely knew what to make of the abrupt announcement. The streets of Havana remained quiet.

But even before Castro's resignation, things had started to shift under the surface. A new generation of Cubans had started to give voice to their anger and frustration in ways unthinkable just a few years ago. According to some estimates, more than half of Cuba's population are between 15 and 45 years of age, and to them it hardly matters whether Fidel's brother, Raúl, is formally chosen as his successor this week, or whether another aging Communist gets the nod. Young Cubans are starting to publicly demand that the regime make tangible improvements in their lives. Their wish lists are decidedly apolitical. Instead of pining for democracy, most are focused on things foreign peers take for granted: the freedom to travel abroad, unrestricted Internet access, enough disposable income to buy a cell phone or an iPod. "These young students are asking, 'Why are things banned, why are we not allowed to leave the island?'" notes Miriam Leiva, a dissident who once held a high-level post in the Cuban Foreign Ministry.

Many have fled. An estimated 77,000 Cubans immigrated to the United States during a two-year period ending last September, the largest exodus from the island since the early 1970s. A disproportionate share of those refugees were teenagers or twentysomethings. "Young people are fed up," says Julia Núñez Pacheco, the wife of Adolfo Fernández Sainz, a jailed independent journalist whose 32-year-old daughter, Joana, left Cuba last year to join her husband in Miami. "Many are escaping, either by hurling themselves into the sea on rafts or by arranging marriages of convenience with foreigners."

But symptoms of mounting discontent are appearing at home, too. Last November, the rape of a young woman at Santiago University triggered a wave of student protest over appalling living conditions and other long-standing grievances. Students gathered more than 5,000 signatures on a petition demanding greater autonomy from Havana's bureaucracy. Then, in January, students at the prestigious University of Information Sciences met with Ricardo Alarcón, the long-time president of Cuba's rubber-stamp national parliament. One student boldly told him that last month's legislative elections had been a sham, since all the candidates had come from the ruling party. Another asked Alarcón what he should say to his peers who yearn to go abroad, adding that he himself wanted to visit a monument in Bolivia to revolutionary icon Ernesto (Che) Guevara. The whole exchange was clandestinely filmed and circulated within days, showing a flustered Alarcón unable to respond to the challenges.

Many of the students in this now celebrated tête à tête were the privileged sons and daughters of the Communist Party's *nomenklatura*, suggesting that youth discontent is rising to the very top of Cuban society. These youngsters came of age in the so-called Special Period, an era of extreme belt-tightening beginning in the early 1990s, when the regime tottered on the brink of collapse after the fall of the Soviet Union. The Special Period put to rest any remaining traces of idealism in Cuba. Those reared in that era saw nothing but food shortages, a decaying public health-care system and the prospect of a $17-a-month job at the end of their studies.

In some ways, 32-year-old Yoani Sánchez is typical. "Unlike our parents, we never believed in anything," she says. "Our defining characteristic is cynicism, but that's a double-edged sword. It protects you from crushing disappointment, but it paralyzes you from doing anything." Yet Sánchez, at least, has done something. In April, she started a groundbreaking blog, *Generacion Y*, that delivers stinging barbs about the day-to-day hassles of life in Cuba: the food shortages at her 12-year-old son's school; the daunting difficulties facing a young couple who want to move out of their parents' households and get their own apartment. Sánchez has become a torchbearer for her generation, and roughly one-fourth of the 800,000 hits her site received last month came from within the island. "I want to see how far we can push the walls of this regime," she says.

To some extent, the rise in dissent is the result of Raúl Castro's policies. Soon after he assumed effective power in the summer of 2006, he called on Cubans to denounce corruption and devise innovative cures for the island's many ills. The state-run newspaper *Juventud Rebelde* (Rebel Youth) took the lead in running investigative stories exposing petty crimes, and then went further by explaining how these crimes were a direct result of "systemic" flaws in the socialist economic model. In allowing such criticism, Raúl seemed to be signaling the time had come for sweeping change. Then nothing happened. Raúl cautiously stayed the course, taking no concrete steps to open the state-dominated economy or encourage greater private initiative and investment. No senior officials were publicly held accountable for incompetence, apart from the country's transportation minister, and the elder Castro seemed to act as a brake on Raúl's plans to reform the island's economy along Chinese lines. In a high-profile speech last summer, Raúl acknowledged the painfully obvious: salaries were too low, food production and distribution were dysfunctional, and the system was full of problems that needed to be addressed. But he was unable to do anything about these woes.

Yet the Communists' lock on power remains strong. Fidel's resignation signals no immediate change in government policy, much less an overhaul. Cuba's disenchanted youth have no organized means for expressing their grievances. None took to the streets in the wake of Fidel's resignation to test the government's patience. "You're starting to see more and more examples of dissidence, but they are still not very organized or united," says Laura Pollán, a human rights activist. But it's a start, and the emergence of dynamic youth protest movements has often breathed new life into dispirited oppositions. How long will it take? No one knows, but the answer might surprise even the country's most optimistic young protesters.

| "When they talk about 'reform' here [in Cuba], they never really mean it."

Dictatorship in Cuba Will Continue

The Economist

Although Cuba has undertaken a number of reforms, the following viewpoint from the Economist *asserts that economic and political conditions in the country have not really changed. Instead, corruption and opposition to liberalization have undermined reforms. In addition, the military is playing an increasing role in the economy and politics of the country. Finally, the continuing influence of Fidel Castro has acted as a brake on efforts to change the rigid Communist system of the island. The* Economist *is one of the world's leading magazines on financial affairs and politics.*

As you read, consider the following questions:

1. How many different self-employment occupations are allowed by the Cuban government?

2. What does the viewpoint assert is the tax rate for private businesses in Cuba?

"Trying to Make the Sums Add Up; Reform in Cuba," *The Economist*, vol. 397, no. 8708, November 13, 2010, p. 44. Copyright © 2010 by The Economist. All rights reserved. Reproduced by permission.

3. What is Cuba's official unemployment rate, according to the viewpoint?

On the rare occasions when Cuba's political leaders want to signal a change of direction, or even just reaffirm existing policies, they do so by calling a congress of the ruling Communist Party. Traditionally, these get-togethers were held every five years or so. But the most recent one took place in 1997. Since then, economic problems, the illness that led to Fidel Castro relinquishing the presidency in 2006, and palpable indecision have led to the repeated postponement of what would be the sixth congress. Many Cubans had assumed it would never happen.

Reforms or Formalities?

Now, at last, Raúl Castro, who replaced his elder brother and was formally named as president in 2008, has summoned the congress for late April [2011] to "make fundamental decisions on how to modernise the Cuban economic model". The announcement comes shortly after the government revealed plans to lay off at least 500,000 state workers and encourage more people to seek self-employment or form co-operatives. The congress will approve new "guidelines for socio-economic policy" set out in a 32-page booklet released this week [November 2010].

So are the Castro brothers, in the twilight of their lives, preparing to lead Cuba towards a mixed economy, similar to that of China? Or are these reforms just short-term, reversible measures, designed to mitigate an acute shortage of cash? The government's recently published list of 178 now-permitted lines of self-employment makes disappointing reading for those who hope for radical reform. If a Communist bureaucrat was asked to present to his superiors a document identifying areas of private enterprise that posed no threat to the state, this would be it.

Cubans can now legally work for themselves as a clown, a button sewer or a fancy-dress dancer (in the costume of a 1940s Cuban crooner, Beny Moré, the list bizarrely specifies). Repairing furniture is allowed; selling it is not. But the list also includes more conventional trades such as building and plumbing. State media have stressed that self-employment should from now on be considered an acceptable way of life, and those that choose it will no longer be "stigmatised". Even so, the guidelines insist that the self-employed will not be allowed to "accumulate property".

One way of interpreting the changes is that rather than creating new opportunities, they merely legalise what was already a widespread informal economy of clandestine private enterprise. Cubans working for themselves will now have to pay taxes, ranging from 25% to 50%. But allowing widespread private businesses requires a host of other changes.

New wholesale outlets will be set up where supplies can be bought. The self-employed will be able to hire staff beyond the family. That is a big change: since the 1960s the use of the words "employee" and "employer" has been strongly discouraged. No longer will wages be capped. Individuals will be allowed to rent, buy and sell their homes.

Past Reforms

Many Cubans remain sceptical. Plenty remember Cuba's first, limited opening to private enterprise in the 1990s (following the fourth party congress, in 1991), when people were allowed to let out rooms and run their own restaurants. Briefly, such businesses thrived. But as soon as government finances improved, as cheap Venezuelan oil partly replaced vanished Soviet largesse, the authorities stopped issuing new licences for self-employment and suffocated family businesses with draconian taxes and endless bureaucracy.

"When they talk about 'reform' here, they never really mean it," says Evelyn, a biology student in Havana. After half a century of life under the Castros, many Cubans have convinced themselves that nothing will ever change. They have become experts at making daily ends meet and not pondering the future. They may be in for a shock.

Cubans' wages are low ($20–30 a month at the unofficial exchange rate) and they have to augment the state ration book in expensive farmers' markets. But the state always guaranteed them jobs, workplace perks, free health care and education, and heavily subsidised housing and transport. Now it is struggling to do so. On top of the long-standing inefficiencies of central planning and the difficulties caused by the American economic embargo have come other blows, including devastating hurricanes in 2008 and fewer tourists because of the world recession. The government has repeatedly defaulted on hard-currency payments.

Raúl Castro takes the view that Cuba can no longer afford the bloated and paternalistic state he inherited from Fidel, and that the state's payroll should be linked to productivity. Government economists calculate that 1m [million] workers, or one in four of those employed by the state, are surplus to requirements. The first layoffs have begun, with several hundred redundancies in the ministry buildings which surround Havana's Plaza de la Revolución.

Officially, unemployment is still only 1.7%. But wander through the capital, and aside from many people hanging around doing nothing, beggars are ever more common. There is a new plea from those asking passing foreigners for money: "There is no work here." As well as cutting spending on education and health, Mr Castro plans to phase out the ration book, replacing it with targeted help.

The calling of the party congress marks the culmination of a four-year debate among Cuba's leaders. Raúl Castro and his allies have clearly won it, against the more doctrinaire officials promoted by Fidel Castro after he abandoned the limited opening of the 1990s. Fidel Castro's health has improved this

The Government and the Cuban Economy

ARTICLE 16. The state organizes, directs and controls the economic life of the nation according to a plan that guarantees the programmed development of the country, with the purpose of strengthening the socialist system, of increasingly satisfying the material and cultural needs of society and of citizens, of promoting the flourishing of human beings and their integrity, and of serving the progress and security of the country.

The workers of all branches of the economy and of the other spheres of social life have an active and conscious participation in the elaboration and execution of the production and development plans.

Constitution of the Republic of Cuba, 1992.

year. But in his public appearances, and in rambling essays read out on the evening news, he has stuck rigidly to comments on world affairs, not domestic issues.

Raúl's victory has been reflected in a gradual shuffling of the government lineup. Only three ministers appointed by Fidel remain in office, and none hold economic jobs. Last to go was Yadira Garcia Vera, sacked as minister of basic industry in September after being publicly accused of poor management.

Victory for the Decentralisers

Raúl, who was previously defence minister, has brought in army officers to do many jobs. The army is Cuba's most efficient institution and has played a big role in the tourist industry since the 1990s. The armed forces' holding company, called GAESA, has emerged as the dominant force in the economy. It is run by Raúl's son-in-law, Colonel Luis Alberto Rodriguez

[López Callejas]. A shadowy figure who speaks English with an impeccable upper-class British accent (which he says he picked up from his KGB [Soviet national security agency] tutors while a student in the Soviet Union), he boasts that his organisation controls 40% of the Cuban economy.

That share looks set to grow. Colonel Hector Oroza [Busutin], formerly the number two at GAESA, was recently put in charge of another state conglomerate, CIMEX, replacing its civilian director. CIMEX is Cuba's biggest company, turning over more than $1 billion; among other things, it processes remittances from Cubans abroad and rents property to foreigners.

The new guidelines promise to intensify the decentralisation of the economy that Raúl favours (and Fidel opposed), granting wide autonomy to state companies. They will be expected to pay their own way—and liquidated if they do not. They may be freer to set up joint ventures with foreign companies, in new "special development zones" aimed at boosting job creation.

Seemingly in preparation for this, many companies have been purged. Managers at Habanos, a cigar maker, have been interrogated over claims that $60m is missing. In September Pedro Alvarez, the former boss of Alimport, which handles food imports from the United States, was arrested at his home and taken away in handcuffs. Several officials at the ministry in charge of oil and nickel production are said to have been jailed after being found guilty of taking, and offering, bribes. "Raúl's men have always been suspicious of some of the civilians who run Cuban businesses," says a businessman in Havana. "Now they seem to be getting rid of them all."

The guidelines fail to join up all the dots of the new economic picture, but together with other recent announcements they do sketch out Raúl's vision for his country: powerful state companies run by trusted army officers, an attempt to tax and regulate the black market by allowing self-employment, and setting wages, prices and employment according to results and productivity. Social provision will increasingly be the job of local party officials. The ultimate aim is to boost exports and reduce reliance on imports, and to unify Cuba's twin currencies of worthless domestic pesos and stronger "convertible" ones.

The big unanswered question concerns the succession. The party congress will be followed by a separate conference to discuss internal political matters, at which clues may be offered. Hidden away in some quiet streets of the capital are once-famous names tipped as future leaders. They now live in obscurity. Roberto Robaina, a former foreign minister, whiles away his time painting watercolours. Felipe Pérez Roque, another former foreign minister, is said to work as an electrician. Carlos Lage [Dávila], de facto prime minister until last year, is believed to be practising medicine again. Perhaps Colonel Rodriguez is the dauphin now. Or maybe the Castros will make no succession arrangements.

Either way, whoever takes over will inherit a system in which, for the first time, there is a small but real place for private enterprise. And stopping small businesses from growing may prove harder than preventing them from being set up at all.

Periodical and Internet Sources Bibliography

The following articles have been selected to supplement the diverse views presented in this chapter.

Keith Bowers	"Inside the Secret State," *New Scientist*, vol. 216, no. 2892, November 24, 2012.
Bruce Cumings	"The Kims' Three Bodies: Communism and Dynastic Succession in North Korea," *Current History*, vol. 111, no. 746, September 2012.
The Economist	"Reform in Cuba: Raúl the Pragmatist," November 11, 2010.
Mark Farmaner	"Burma: A Normal Dictatorship?," *World Today*, vol. 67, no. 11, December 2011.
Cynthia Gorney	"Cuba's New Now," *National Geographic*, vol. 222, no. 5, November 2012.
Christine Hong	"The First Year of Peace on the Korean Peninsula," *Foreign Policy in Focus*, October 11, 2012.
G. Philip Hughes	"Cuban Reforms Not Enough," *U.S. News Weekly*, February 24, 2012.
Rob Long	"From the Twitter Feed of @youthcaptain, the Next Leader of the Democratic People's Republic of Korea ...," *National Review Online*, May 16, 2011.
Nancy Macdonald and Gabriela Perdomo	"Foreign Business in Cuba: Beware the Dangerous Embrace," *Maclean's*, August 8, 2012.
Bill Powell	"Meet Kim Jong Un," *Time*, February 27, 2012.
Yoani Sánchez	"Country for Old Men," *Foreign Policy*, November 2011.

CHAPTER 3

Are Select Democracies Becoming Dictatorships?

Chapter Preface

As noted in the previous chapter in the case of Myanmar, democracies can transition to dictatorships. Often during times of chaos or internal strife, people are willing to allow a ruler to assume broad powers if he or she can provide peace and stability. In Latin America, there is the tradition of the *caudillo*—leader or chief—or military dictator. The *caudillo* is usually a military leader who becomes dictator during a time of crisis and restores order. However, once in office, dictators tend to entrench themselves and seek more and more power and authority. They do not have limits on their power and are not accountable to the people for their decisions. One common result is that regimes that come to power to end corruption typically become very dishonest and corrupt themselves, prompting new crises and instability.

After the end of the Cold War, Russia rejected its authoritarian Communist government and attempted to create a democratic government. The country had little experience with democracy, and the political, social, and economic transition was a difficult one. Many Russians became worse off economically than they were under the Communist regime. Vladimir Putin was elected president of Russia in 2000 and reelected in 2004. The Russian constitution limited presidents to two consecutive terms, so after leaving office in 2008, Putin became prime minister of the country, only to be elected president again in 2012 in balloting that was criticized by domestic and foreign observers. Putin's critics charge that he is undermining Russian democracy and creating a stealth dictatorship. However, under Putin the Russian economy has stabilized and grown considerably, even if the benefits of that growth have not been uniformly distributed.

Venezuela suffered from considerable instability in the 1980s and 1990s with a series of attempted coups. One of the coups was led by an army colonel, Hugo Chávez, who was arrested but pardoned in 1994. Chávez became increasingly popular over the next four years by promising to transform the country. He was elected president in 1998. He then oversaw revisions to the constitution that gave the presidency more power and authority. Chávez survived a coup in 2002 and went on to further strengthen the presidency. He was re-elected president in 2006 and 2012. Opponents of Chávez charge that he is creating a dictatorship, while his supporters laud his social programs and efforts to help the poor.

Since independence in 1960, Madagascar went through four different constitutions. Following a disputed election in 2001, Marc Ravalomanana became president and the country entered a period of peace and stability. However, Ravalomanana was forced from power in 2009 and replaced by Andry Rajoelina, bringing into question the future of democracy in Madagascar.

The viewpoints in the following chapter examine the prospects for dictatorship in countries such as Venezuela and Madagascar, two countries with limited democratic histories, as well as Kenya, which has shifted from democracy to dictatorship and back to democracy again. The authors analyze the tactics and strategies used by leaders in these countries to enhance their power and whether those actions will lead to dictatorship.

[Editor's note: Venezuelan president Hugo Chávez died on March 5, 2013, and Vice President Nicolás Maduro took over the presidential powers and duties until elections could be held.]

"In no sense does this situation benefit Venezuelans from any social group. [Chávez] has caused too much chaos and unrest for the country to develop."

Chávez: From Hero to Tyrant

Alice O'Keeffe

Alice O'Keeffe argues in the following viewpoint that Venezuelan president Hugo Chávez has increased his own power and authority by pitting Venezuelans against each other. As a result, the country has become increasingly polarized and plagued by violence. Meanwhile, Chávez has suppressed voices critical of his rule, especially among the media and student groups, O'Keeffe maintains. She concludes that the Venezuelan president has demonized his opponents and undermined the democratic institutions within the country. O'Keeffe is a journalist and writer for the New Statesman *magazine.*

[Editor's note: Venezuelan president Hugo Chávez died on March 5, 2013, and Vice President Nicolás Maduro took over the presidential powers and duties until elections could be held.]

Alice O'Keeffe, "Chávez: From Hero to Tyrant," *New Statesman*, vol. 136, no. 4853, July 16, 2007, pp. 28, 30–31. Copyright © 2007 by New Statesman. All rights reserved. Reproduced by permission.

As you read, consider the following questions:

1. From 2000 to 2007, when this viewpoint was written, how many more Venezuelans were living in the United States, as the author estimates?

2. According to the viewpoint, what is the number one cause of death among men between the ages of fifteen and twenty-five in Venezuela?

3. With what does Hugo Chávez intend to replace independent student unions?

"*El Presidente" was returned to power on a wave of popular support after the failed coup of 2002. But now his divisive policies are turning friends into enemies. Some claim his strident rhetoric risks provoking civil war. Alice O'Keeffe reports from Caracas.*

In the corner of a toy shop in downtown Caracas lays a dusty pile of battery-operated talking Hugo Chávez dolls. *El Presidente* was dressed in full military regalia and, at the touch of a button, would deliver a speech on the Bolivarian revolution. "Sale: half-price," said a notice propped up on top. The sales assistant gave them a disparaging glance. "I wish I could buy them all," she said conspiratorially, "so I could burn them."

One thing you can say with certainty about Venezuela's president is that he provokes strong emotions. People in Caracas offer their political opinions almost before introducing themselves. On my first foray into the city's streets, I asked a bookseller where I could buy a map, and he gripped my arm fervently before replying: "There is only one thing you need to know about Caracas, and that is that we are revolutionaries." The whole population has been politicised; it has also been polarised into two ferociously hostile camps, Chavistas and the derogatorily named opposition of "*esqualidos*" ("squalid people"). The tone of debate is so angry that the situation is often described as a "cold civil war".

With a power-crazed Chávez at the helm, the fear is that it may not remain cold.

Like many cities in Latin America, Caracas is characterised by the sharp contrast between its spacious and tranquil affluent areas and the poor, gang-ridden barrios that sprawl up the surrounding hills. Since the attempted right-wing coup that briefly deposed Chávez in 2002, a dangerous face-off between the two has been evolving. Carlos Caridad Montero, a Caracas-based filmmaker, took me to see one of the city's front lines: the motorway that runs between Petare, the largest barrio, and the middle-class area of Terrazas del Ávila. On one side of the road, the brick shacks of Petare are stacked on top of each other like brightly coloured Lego. On the other stands a set of grim, if slightly better-heeled, tower blocks.

"Everyone in these blocks is armed in case the gangs from Petare try to invade the area," Carlos told me. "And on the other side, you have the gangs, who are also heavily armed. In Petare, they call the people who live on this side gringos, as if they were American rather than Venezuelan."

William Ury, a conflict resolution expert at Harvard, identifies three typical symptoms of a country on the brink of civil war. The first is that the population begins to arm itself; the second is that each side begins to dehumanise and impute evil intentions to the other; and the third is the politicisation of the media. Contemporary Venezuela has each of these conditions in abundance. Ury suggests that the key to defusing the threat is to strengthen the "third side": those organisations or people who empathise with both sides of the conflict and will encourage others to resolve their differences nonviolently.

The Chávez regime is making it increasingly difficult for anyone to remain on the "third side". Carlos has good left-wing credentials (he trained in Cuba). He is broadly sympathetic to Chávez, but is also concerned about the effects of political polarisation. However, working for Villa del Cine, the year-old government-backed cinema organisation, he will be expected to produce what the minister of culture has termed "cinema with an ideological tendency". Films perceived to be critical of the government or to cast Venezuela in a bad light will not be welcomed. "I co-operate because I believe there is important work to be done that does not involve criticising Chávez," he said. "The problem is that as soon as I tell people who I am working for they assume my work is 'propaganda'. You are forced on to one side or the other."

Another prominent film director, Alejandro Bellame, told me that "it is true we still have nominal freedom of speech. But now what you say has consequences. If you dare to criticise, more and more doors will be closed to you. This system rewards loyalty above talent or hard work."

Despite the divisive revolutionary rhetoric, many middle-class professionals support Chávez's determination to integrate poorer communities into Venezuelan politics. Yanay Arrocha, a publicist working for the recently closed anti-Chávez television station Radio Caracas Televisión (RCTV), told me: "The achievement of this government has been that the great majority of people now discuss politics and are interested in the nation. Poor people understand that they have rights, and rich people understand that they have a responsibility, and that there are problems to resolve." But the price has been a painful erosion of common values, she said. "The attitude that is transmitted from the top is that if you think differently from me, you are my enemy."

The social breakdown in Venezuela makes its presence felt in many ways, not least the 80 per cent increase since 2000 in the number of Venezuelans—mainly the educated professionals any developing country desperately needs—living in the United States. Street crime and delinquency have also grown alarmingly: According to the United Nations, Venezuela recently overtook Brazil in having the highest rate of gun-related violence in the world among nations not at war.

Freedom of Speech in Venezuela

The gradual erosion of press freedom in Venezuela continued in 2010. The media landscape featured political intimidation by government officials and state-owned media in their opinion programs, laws restricting the exercise of basic human rights, systematic judicial and administrative harassment of opposition outlets, economic threats against independent media, and physical attacks against journalists amid a worsening climate of common criminality.

"Freedom of the Press 2011: Venezuela,"
Freedom House, October 27, 2011.

In Caracas, homicide has become the most common cause of death for men between 15 and 25. Much of the violence is contained in the poorer barrios, although "express" kidnappings and carjackings are a significant preoccupation across the city. "We have been subjected to a political rhetoric which in some way justifies the use of violence as a response to poverty," said Bellame. "What Chávez has not grasped is that you can't create solidarity by decree."

Chaos and Unrest

Until lately, opposition to Chávez was characterised as "right-wing" or, in the terminology used by the president and his supporters, "imperialist". Since May, when the government shut down RCTV, the country's most popular channel, this has been changing fast. The charges against it were of anti-government bias, in particular its refusal to air news of the pro-Chávez protests that brought him back to power after the 2002 coup. However, RCTV was predominantly an entertainment channel, and showed some of the nation's favourite soap operas, or "*novelas*". In a young country, its 53-year broadcasting history gave it national heritage status; one acquaintance described it as "part of our collective consciousness". Polls showed that 70 per cent of Venezuelans disagreed with the decision to take it off the air.

RCTV has been replaced by TVes (pronounced *té vès*, or "you see yourself"), a government channel that has the apparently laudable aim of moving away from a Western, consumerist agenda and reflecting the "real" Venezuela. But when I tuned in at prime time on a Saturday evening, it was broadcasting an hour-long programme about the armed forces, encouraging conscription to the reserves. An army general was explaining, over footage of Iraqi insurgents waving guns, that ordinary Venezuelans had to be trained in tactics of "asymmetrical resistance".

"What the country needs now is union, complete union between the population and the armed forces," he said. The journalist conducting the interview smiled and nodded.

"Chávez is, above all, a military man," explained Ivo Hernández, a professor of political science, when I went to see him at the Simón Bolívar public university on the outskirts of Caracas. "Politics for him is a battle: There are no greys—just black and white. The idea of doing things consensually doesn't enter his head. In no sense does this situation benefit Venezuelans from any social group. He has caused too much chaos and unrest for the country to develop." The university itself is buzzing with dissent, with "freedom of speech" graffiti daubed on walls and cars throughout the leafy complex. Students in yellow T-shirts run around putting up posters advertising rallies and protest marches.

The RCTV shutdown has been the catalyst for an important new wave of opposition, spearheaded by a national student movement. Almost daily, students have been marching through the streets of the capital, protesting against curbs on freedom of speech and, crucially, on the independence of universities (Chávez has announced plans to replace independent student unions with government-friendly "Popular Student Power" councils). The protesters—who are from public and private universities alike, and therefore from diverse social backgrounds—do not use the emotive anti-Chávez rhetoric employed by the right-wing opposition. Instead, they promote the idea of "national reconciliation", which they symbolise by painting their hands white.

I attended a student rally at a baseball stadium in central Caracas. Thousands of young people from around the country were packed in, waving Venezuelan flags and chanting, "We are students, not coup-plotters." Sindy López, a fresh-faced 19-year-old from Simón Bolívar University, was there with her friend Maria González.

"When they closed RCTV, we really got desperate, and furious about the lack of freedom of expression and diversity of thought," she said. "We realised we could not let it carry on. It is not like the president says—I'm not from the elite; my family doesn't even own a house. I just can't see this happen to my country."

Chávez has responded to the protests by claiming that those involved are "representatives of the international bourgeoisie" who are being manipulated by the right. He called on those living in the barrios to "defend our revolution from this fascist aggression"—a comment that was interpreted by many RCTV supporters as an incitement to attack.

"We have been trying to make our voices heard nonviolently," said one protester. "The problem is that the president wants violence." So far, the marches have been peaceful.

The students have been dubbed the "2007 generation" by the Venezuelan media, and have become a focus for protest from other pockets of opposition, including journalists. Their agenda centres on inclusive politics; having grown up under Chávez, they are well aware that they will not succeed without the support of poor communities. They are attempting to create a dialogue, with students who live in the barrios being encouraged to set up discussions and consultations that feed back into the movement.

"Every one of us needs to bring the debate to their work, their family, their barrio," said one of the student leaders, Stalin González. "We don't want to impose any idea or ideology on anyone. All we want is for every Venezuelan to have a say in how we construct this country."

Chávez will have to listen to their message—and soon.

> "*[A researcher] points to massive decreases in extreme poverty, gains in literacy, declining unemployment, and a general reorientation of state priorities toward public welfare under Chávez.*"

Hugo Chávez Is Not Changing Venezuela into a Dictatorship

Bhaskar Sunkara

In the following viewpoint, the author examines the impact of President Hugo Chávez's economic and social programs on the Venezuelan people. Like other populist Latin American leaders, author Bhaskar Sunkara asserts, Chávez has endeavored to expand the presence of economic cooperatives as an alternative to capitalism. These systems can promote democracy within companies, Sunkara argues, and spread the values of the regime into the economic sphere; they also serve as a means to reduce the power of elites within society. Sunkara is a writer and the founding editor of the leftist journal Jacobin.

[Editor's note: Venezuelan president Hugo Chávez died on March 5, 2013, and Vice President Nicolás Maduro took over the presidential powers and duties until elections could be held.]

Bhaskar Sunkara, "Hugo Chávez as Postmodern Perón," *Dissent*, vol. 59, no. 1, Winter 2012, pp. 22–24. Reprinted with permission of the University of Pennsylvania Press.

As you read, consider the following questions:

1. When was the Mondragon Corporation founded?

2. According to the viewpoint, what has been the failure rate of cooperatives?

3. To which Latin American leader does Sunkara assert Hugo Chávez is often compared?

What benefits has Hugo Chávez's populist administration brought to the Venezuelan people? In a controversial 2008 *Foreign Affairs* article, "An Empty Revolution," Venezuelan economist Francisco Rodríguez argues that the regime has not improved the quality of life in the country in any substantial way, it hasn't actually given greater priority to welfare than past governments had done, and its claims of poverty reduction are overstated. Human development indicators have improved in some regards, he writes, but this has always been the case during commodity booms. Rodríguez even disputes the most frequently lauded achievement of the Bolivarian Revolution, the *Barrio Adentro* health services program that aims to provide cradle-to-grave medical services in poor communities. In rebuttal, Mark Weisbrot of the Center for Economic and Policy Research criticizes Rodríguez's use of statistics and points to massive decreases in extreme poverty, gains in literacy, declining unemployment, and a general reorientation of state priorities toward public welfare under Chávez.

The Debate Over Chávez's Impact

Weisbrot and Rodríguez's dispute is not unique. Debating the success of Venezuelan social programs and the methodology used to measure economic and social indicators has consumed many observers. But though the establishment of new social and economic rights and the security that might be afforded to the Venezuelan poor by an effective welfare system should not be dismissed, socialism—in the Marxian [referring

117

to the theories of Karl Marx] mold, at least—has historically been more about redistributing power than wealth. It is this fundamental altering of human relations and the social structures that mediate them that intrigue many defenders of Chávez's "Bolivarian Revolution."

Like Lincoln Steffens, who on return from the newly formed Soviet Union declared, "I have been over into the future and it works," some have seen in Venezuelan cooperatives, community councils, and co-managed firms the seedlings of a socialist society. The type of intervention needed for a detailed analysis of these new institutions is beyond the scope of this [viewpoint], but one particular claim—about the explosion of Venezuelan cooperatives and their anti-capitalist character—deserves examination. It provides insights relevant to the entire radical populist experiment.

"A Cornerstone of Socialist Construction"

Cooperatives have long captured the imagination of the Left. The Mondragon Corporation, a network based in the Basque territory and often held up as a model of the cooperative movement, is a well-known example. It represents what is perhaps the best that can be accomplished in a worker-controlled archipelago surrounded by a capitalist sea. Since its founding in 1956, the federally organized corporation has sprawled far beyond the town of Mondragon; today, it employs over 85,000 and is one of the leading business groups in Spain. The complex is proof that efficient enterprises, even corporations with tens of thousands of employees, can be structured democratically, and it suggests that a dynamic economy can thrive without capitalists. With the success of a worker-owned management research center, the entrepreneurial role of "productive" capital has been socialized. The corporation's banks provide capital and technical expertise for expanding the existing cooperatives and adding new affiliates. The whole enterprise is a prototype for civic investment at a time when so many are discontented with the global banking system.

Yet it is impossible to ignore the limits of this venture. As Sharryn Kasmir notes in *The Myth of Mondragón*, there is something striking about the way Mondragon fits with the spirit of post-'68 capitalism. She sees the cooperative's workplace complementing, not challenging, a flexible, "team oriented" . . . capitalist order. Kasmir cites survey data indicating that the majority of workers don't feel that their firms actually belong to them. And, not surprisingly, the corporation as a whole remains hostage to the world market. Still, the experiment suggests that the masters of industry are replaceable after all.

Venezuela, a country with state funding and logistical support for the cooperative sector, would seem poised to replicate the success of Mondragon on a large scale. The number of cooperatives registered in Venezuela has risen from the hundreds to the hundreds of thousands over the past decade. Analyses from the Western Left have designated them an antibureaucratic form of socialization far superior to state-directed nationalization. They constitute, from this view, a cornerstone of socialist construction in the country.

However, the reality beneath the rhetoric of "endogenous development" is less than inspiring. Out of the more than 220,000 registered cooperatives, only 70,000 are active—a failure rate of 70 percent. The ones that have survived, far from serving as vehicles of worker empowerment, have in some respects institutionalized underground-economy work without improving conditions. Since they are supposedly equal "partners" in a firm, groups of cooperative members who feel exploited within their workplace cannot engage in industrial action. This status as "self-employed associates" rather than "workers" also means they are exempt from national labor laws governing basic protections such as minimum wage requirements. These features are attractive to large capitalist firms that outsource work to cooperatives—many of them staffed by unemployed ex-union members—in order to minimize their reliance on combative permanent workers.

The trend is not limited to the private sector. Many cooperatives rely on state contracts, replacing public sector unionized jobs with more precarious contracted labor. In a widely cited case, the . . . former mayor of Caracas, Juan Barreto, allowed cooperatives to compete for municipal contracts. Several unions were forced to dissolve under the competitive pressure and reorganize as a series of small cooperatives with no collective bargaining rights. . . .

The Third Way

For all its contradictions, the Mondragon initiative grew from below. The Chávez government has promoted cooperatives from above through a restrictive legal framework that undercuts existing working-class organization and closes off opportunities for self-emancipation. Nor is this project a novel one. Stripped of their relationship to an independent workers' movement, cooperatives were welcomed by [dictator Francisco] Franco in Spain and [dictator Benito] Mussolini in Italy, regimes that found nonconfrontational relations between labor and management a complement to corporatism. Presently they subsist happily in large swathes of the capitalist world, sometimes offered up by "third way" think tanks as a half-way house on the road to privatization.

But the relationship between Chávez and his supporters is complex and dialectical. Even though—through an influx of state credit, training programs, and moral exhortations—the cooperative project has been initiated from the top down, the momentum pushing the wider Bolivarian movement has come from struggles from below—political activity that had reached a nadir before Chávez's election. This is an important difference between the classical and radical populist eras. [Former Argentinean president] Juan Perón—with whom Chávez is inevitably compared—and his cohorts co-opted a rising Left. Chávez has seemingly resurrected one and has at times struggled to keep up with the forces he helped unleash. The Bolivarian Circles represent with exquisite precision the ethos of the revolution: These community councils were organized in an attempt to bury the state deep into civil society, to bypass potentially hostile local elected officials, and to dole out patronage directly from the center. They are, as Nikolas Kozloff puts it, at once "anti-democratic, creating a kind of vertical dependency around the cult figure of Chávez" and a real terrain of democratic deliberation. Acknowledging this paradox is key to a sober understanding of radical populism and its contradictions.

In failing health, facing an emboldened opposition, Chávez's hold on power is precarious. The question now is whether Chavismo [referring to the political movement that supports Chávez] can survive after he is gone. Millions have been politicized, but to what end? Latin American populism has grown from poverty and inequity. But even in its newest form, whatever the utopian rhetoric, it remains incapable either of efficiently managing the capitalist state or offering a post-capitalist alternative.

"*Nearly every president in the history of Madagascar ... has changed the constitution to suit his needs.*"

Democracies in Africa Are Becoming Dictatorships

Jerome Y. Bachelard and Richard R. Marcus

In the following viewpoint, Jerome Y. Bachelard and Richard R. Marcus contend that democracy is being eroded in Madagascar. The viewpoint examines the recent history of the country and the efforts to reform its political system. A coup in 2009 deposed the democratically elected president and ushered in a period of uncertainty as international groups endeavored to negotiate a compromise. Bachelard is a research fellow at the Institute for Social and Economic Research and Policy and the Center for the Study of Development Strategies at Columbia University. Marcus is an associate professor and the director of International Studies at California State University, Long Beach.

As you read, consider the following questions:

1. As the authors report, how many people were killed when security forces opened fire on demonstrators in February 2009?

Jerome Y. Bachelard and Richard R. Marcus, "Countries at the Crossroads 2011: Madagascar," Freedom House, 2011. Reproduced by permission.

2. What organization negotiated a power-sharing agreement in Madagascar in 2011?

3. Which article of the Madagascar constitution allows the president to rule by decree during an emergency?

In March 2009, after weeks of street protests, Andry Rajoelina took control of Madagascar through a military-backed and unconstitutional seizure of power. The ousting of President Marc Ravalomanana was a large step backwards for the country's already backsliding democratization, embroiling the country in a political crisis that remains unresolved.

Street demonstrations have long been principal drivers of political change in Madagascar. The events of 2009 should thus be considered in historical context. In 1947 Madagascar experienced one of the most significant anti-colonial insurrections in the world. An estimated 100,000 people died in the conflict, and the memory of 1947 still plays a cardinal role in shaping Malagasy political culture. All demonstrations since have been urban. When institutions have failed to provide the forum necessary for the legal contestation of ideas, some people have taken to the streets to bring about change.

New Constitution

In 1991, over 100,000 people staged demonstrations and strikes to force President Didier Ratsiraka to accept a transitional government. This led to the adoption of a new constitution in 1992, and was followed by the election of opposition leader Albert Zafy in multiparty elections in 1993. Ratsiraka was reelected in 1996 after Zafy was impeached.

Official results for the December 2001 elections between Ratsiraka and Marc Ravalomanana, a successful businessman and the popular mayor of Antananarivo, indicated that no candidate won an absolute majority and called for a runoff. Ratsiraka had reportedly used the country's weak electoral institutions to manipulate the results in an attempt to retain power. The population demanded a comparison of the official results with those collected at the ballot stations by a consortium of domestic observers and by Ravalomanana supporters. Hundreds of thousands of people demonstrated, eventually forcing Ratsiraka out of Antananarivo. The country then reached the point of near-Balkanization when Ratsiraka and his partisans established control in his home province of Toamasina and invited the other provinces to establish independent governments. International mediation failed, and Ravalomanana rode the support of part of the army and the ever-growing street demonstrations, which continued for six months. Ratsiraka finally fled for France, and Ravalomanana became president after the majority of the army moved in his favor and defeated Ratsiraka's troops.

During his one and a half terms in office, Ravalomanana conducted significant reforms that were beneficial both to the population as a whole and to his personal interests as the owner of the country's most important private company, the Tiko Group. Reforms included a relatively successful fight against corruption, the strengthening of the judiciary and other state institutions, and the extension of political and economic liberties. Ravalomanana was, however, highly criticized for centralizing power, making decisions alone, and eschewing alternative views and critics. The result was an ever-centralizing hold on power, a narrowing base of confidants and decision makers, a growing reputation for secrecy, and a conflation of business and public interests.

A Power Shift

With the end of a full election cycle in late 2007 came new challenges to President Ravalomanana from opposition leaders, civil society, and even some international donors with whom he had long enjoyed a strong relationship. Ravalomanana was profoundly challenged for quietly entering into a land deal with the South Korean Daewoo [International] Corporation which would have leased 1.3 million hectares (about 18 percent of Madagascar's arable land) and for purchasing "Air Force II" for his use at public expense. The tipping point came on December 13, 2008, when Ravalomanana closed down the private TV station, Viva, owned by the then mayor of Antananarivo, Andry Rajoelina. On January 17, 2009, Rajoelina staged a large rally for the naming of the *Place de la Démocratie* in Antananarivo, which was intended to be an affront to the perceived centralizing and increasingly authoritarian tendencies of President Ravalomanana. Rajoelina served as a lightning rod to a largely marginalized, if disparate, opposition and some 30,000 demonstrators. While support for Ravalomanana was weak, street movements supporting Rajoelina quickly dropped to an estimated 3,000 to 5,000 people daily in Antananarivo, largely because Rajoelina had proclaimed himself in charge of the country's affairs, discrediting his democratic aims. On February 7, 2009, Ravalomanana's presidential guard opened fire on unarmed Rajoelina supporters protesting in front of the presidential palace. An estimated 31 people were killed and more than 200 wounded. This significantly undermined Ravalomanana's legitimacy, but did not necessarily buoy Rajoelina's popularity. On March 17, 2009, under significant pressure, Ravalomanana attempted to hand power over to a military leader. This failed and a group of military mutineers installed Rajoelina in power. Within weeks it became clear that public sentiment challenged Ravalomanana's centralization and his legitimacy while condemning the militancy and patrimony of Rajoelina's rule. This fissure has helped to expose significant structural problems in the Malagasy polity ranging from persistent patterns of personal rule that undermine the institution of the presidency, a significant urban-rural rupture, the persistence of historically entrenched families in the political decision-making process, the failures of decentralization, and the massive divide between those engaged in the export-led growth of a vibrant business economy and the nearly 80 percent rural poor. Today Ravalomanana is in exile in South Africa and Andry Rajoelina has consolidated his rule as the unelected president of the *Haute Autorité de la Transition* (HAT).

Initially the HAT brought together a broad array of political opposition leaders, but over time many of those networks of power have abandoned Rajoelina, and he has become increasingly isolated. Internationally, most donors, including the EU [European Union], the World Bank, the United States, and Norway—but with the notable exception of France—froze their non-humanitarian aid to Madagascar. This is significant, for as of 2008 approximately 70 percent of state revenue came from donor support. The Southern African Development Community (SADC) suspended Madagascar's membership, and the African Union (AU) imposed sanctions against Rajoelina and 108 of his supporters.

Power-Sharing Deal

On August 9, 2009, Rajoelina signed a power-sharing agreement with Ravalomanana, Ratsiraka, and Zafy under international mediation. The deal was broken before the ink was dry, and Rajoelina unilaterally named a new cabinet. Significant international mediation efforts by the UN [United Nations], SADC, the AU, and partnering countries have borne no fruit. On February 4, 2011, SADC mediators proposed a road map to elections that left Rajoelina in power with the caveat that he name a multilateral cabinet. The new transitional unity government named by Rajoelina in March 2011 did not receive backing from the three main opponents, former presidents Ravalomanana, Ratsiraka, and Zafy, and received tepid support from an international community. At the time of writing, the SADC Secretariat had significantly modified the road map written by its mediators and a "take it or leave it" deal was rejected by the HAT. Rajoelina indicated he wanted to move quickly toward elections but was criticized for not meeting the terms of international mediators. SADC moved to block elections.

Since seizing power in 2009, Rajoelina has done little more than attempt to secure his position in power and those of others in his political and business network. He has governed through significantly reduced international aid resources, amidst quickly eroding popular support. Madagascar is facing the threat of state unravel in which the ability to govern across sectors is diminishing.

Nearly every president in the history of Madagascar, including Rajoelina, has changed the constitution to suit his needs. Rajoelina spearheaded a unilateral constitutional convention and national referendum on November 17, 2010. The polls were run in the tense atmosphere of another failed military coup attempt. The constitution officially passed with 74.19 percent support and a participation rate of 52.61 percent despite a call for boycott from the three opposition movement leaders. The civil society monitors, *Comité National d'Observation des Elections* (CNOE), criticized the polls as the worst they had observed in 20 years. The Fourth Republic, which entered into force on December 11, 2010, reduces the minimum age for the president from 40 to 35, allowing 36-year-old Rajoelina to run in the next presidential election. In addition, Article 166 allows him to stay in power until the presidential election takes place, but it does not set a deadline for those elections. Constitutional scholars in Madagascar and abroad have criticized the constitution as a document that obfuscates key elements of the balance of powers while giving more power to an already near-imperial presidential office.

Accountability and Public Elections

The constitution has provided for multiparty elections with universal suffrage since 1992. The 2001 presidential election was initially highly fraudulent, with a clear lack of indepen-

Presidents of Madagascar and Their Terms

President	Term	Reason for Leaving Office
Philibert Tsiranana	1959–1972	Resigned after turning over power to military government.
Gabriel Ramanantsoa	1972–1975	Resigned during widespread demonstrations and strife.
Richard Ratsimandrava	1975	Assassinated.
Gilles Andriamahazo	1975	Resigned after successor was named as head of a military government.
Didier Ratsiraka	1975–1993	Left office after losing election.
Albert Zafy	1993–1996	Resigned after being impeached.
Norbert Ratsirahonana	1996–1997	Left office after losing election.
Didier Ratsiraka	1997–2002	Left office following disputed election and brief civil war.
Marc Ravalomanana	2002–2009	Forced from office by rebellion.
Andry Rajoelina	2009–present	

Complied by editor.

dence both of the National Electoral Council and the High Constitutional Court. The recount conducted in April 2002 yielded results probably much closer to reality than those of the initial tallying, although it is not clear whether Ravalomanana won an absolute majority in the first round.

The 2006 presidential election was relatively free from massive fraud, but some electoral violations were reported. The SADC Election Observer Mission considered the elections inconsistent with regionally established electoral norms. The international observer mission of the Electoral Institute for Sustainable Democracy in Africa (EISA) noted numerous concerns, including polling practices, opaque voters' rolls, a lack of campaign finance information, the perpetuation of a multi-ballot system, an unusually high number of omissions from voter rolls, and errors in identification cards. The CNOE expressed concerns that regional chiefs were withholding distribution of national identification cards in opposition areas to prevent opposition supporters from voting.

There were cases of electoral intimidation in both the 2006 presidential and 2007 legislative elections, including the closing down of opposition headquarters in Tamatave and the arrest of some opposition candidates. Ravalomanana's government prevented Pierrot Rajaonarivelo, Ravalomanana's main challenger in 2006, from returning to Madagascar to run in the election. While Rajaonarivelo claimed that he had committed no crimes, he risked arrest because of accusations by the Ravalomanana government of corruption. Ravalomanana defended the actions, citing possible security concerns if Rajaonarivelo returned.

The multi-ballot system was also highly problematic. Candidates were obliged to pay for and distribute their own ballots, with the possibility of reimbursement if they won at least 10 percent of the votes. This policy, designed to limit sham candidacies, effectively discriminated against candidates with limited financial means. Rajoelina's government changed the electoral code in March 2010 to introduce a single-ballot system. The new electoral code meets every concern expressed by international observers and members of the international community in the lead-up to the 2006 and 2007 elections, but its unilateral imposition and the lack of autonomy of the Independent National Electoral Commission (CENI) it establishes are a continuing area of concern.

The new CENI replaced the National Electoral Council, which was never able to counteract the power of the presidency. The imbalance of power was exacerbated by the High Constitutional Court (HCC), which validated the transfer of full power from Ravalomanana to a military directorate in March 2009, and from that directorate to Rajoelina, even though he was not elected and did not meet the constitutional minimum age for eligibility. The HCC further validated Rajoelina's dissolution of the National Assembly and the Senate, allowing him to rule by decree.

Campaign financing is not regulated, leading to large inequalities between candidates. The dearth of rules makes it unnecessary for candidates to hide the origins of campaign funds. While Ratsiraka belonged to the ruling elite, Ravalomanana largely relied on his own business to finance his political campaigns.

The Organization of Political Power

Not a single political party in Madagascar has ever been a democratic instrument able to recruit new leadership, aggregate interests from various segments of society, and translate them into coherent political programs. They have instead operated as tools for political elites to remain in power and secure sufficient legislative representation. Historically the strongest, Ratsiraka's AREMA party relied on his personal networks and control of state resources to place key allies in office, including many members of his own family, at the national, provincial, and local levels. In the 2001 presidential elections,

Ravalomanana's I Love Madagascar (TIM) party surprised the entire political class by securing, six months after its creation, the largest share of votes in five out of the six provinces. It hence proved that it was possible for a member of Ravalomanana's Merina ethnic group to win nationwide electoral support that cut across social divides. Ravalomanana, unwilling to share power, kept the TIM party under his strict control, silencing alternative voices within the party.

Madagascar is a highly centralized state. The 1998 constitution created six autonomous provinces, a strategy that favors regional allies at the expense of elites in Antananarivo. In 2004, Ravalomanana replaced the provinces with 22 regions controlled by the central government. By law regional chiefs were to be elected, but in practice Ravalomanana appointed them. The 2010 constitution establishes three layers of decentralizations—communes, regions, and provinces—with executive and legislative elections at each level. These elections, however, have yet to be organized, and the autonomy of these decentralized authorities from the central government remains to be seen.

Political power is centralized in the executive. From a legal perspective, the power of the presidency in the 1998–2007 constitution is higher than in Iceland, the European country with the most powerful president in a semi-presidential system, and even higher than in Russia. The 2007 constitutional change increased presidential powers by allowing the president to rule by decree in case of emergency or catastrophe (Art. 100), among other changes. While such a provision existed in the previous constitution, the latter required prior consultation with the presidents of the National Assembly, the Senate, and the HCC (Art. 59). The November 2010 constitution is vague regarding the exact balance of power between the president, legislature, and judiciary. However, given the number of prerogatives attributed to the presidency and the dramatic increase in the presidency's budget while ministry budgets have shrunk, it is likely that presidential powers are even stronger. Article 61 reintroduced the necessity for the president to consult with the presidents of the National Assembly, the Senate, and the HCC before declaring a state of emergency and ruling by decree. In practice, however, this reintroduction has little relevance as Rajoelina dissolved the two parliamentary chambers upon arrival to power.

> "The referendum showed that [Kenya] had genuinely returned to a democratic path and established a strong sense of political plurarlism."

Economic Freedom: Country Studies—Kenya

Democracy Web

Kenya was a democracy after gaining independence from Great Britain. In the following viewpoint, Democracy Web reports that democracy was soon replaced by dictatorship as a series of authoritarian leaders took power. However, in the 2000s, democracy was restored following protests and demonstrations. Kenya continues to face challenges because of the legacy of authoritarian rule, asserts Democracy Web, but it also continues to democratize. Democracy Web is an interactive website that provides comparative political, economic, and social information on countries. It was developed by the Albert Shanker Institute and Freedom House.

As you read, consider the following questions:

1. What group replaced the ruling political party in Kenya in 2002?

"Economic Freedom: Country Studies—Kenya," Democracy Web, 2010. Reproduced by permission.

2. How many Kenyans died, in the author's estimation, during the rebellion against British rule in the 1950s?

3. According to the viewpoint, when was the first peaceful transfer of power in Kenya's postcolonial history?

Summary

Kenya, a middle-sized country of 582,660 square kilometers (47th largest in the world), is located on the eastern coast of Africa. Its port cities served as Muslim trading centers under the control of an Omani dynasty before the country became a colony of Great Britain in the late 19th century. After it achieved independence in 1963, Kenya's early period of democracy devolved into a one-party state by 1969. Although multiparty elections were held beginning in 1992, the ruling party retained power until the opposition National Rainbow Coalition defeated it in 2002.

Kenya's first president, Jomo Kenyatta, adopted policies that improved the overall economy and land distribution, while allowing white colonial residents to retain property rights. Particularly after Kenya became a one-party state in 1969, elite members of the president's Kikuyu ethnic group received preferential treatment in the distribution of wealth, land, and offices, and corruption flourished. Under Kenyatta's successor, who took power in 1978, the economy deteriorated. Once one of Africa's economic success stories, Kenya fell into poverty. In 2006, with a growing population of nearly 35 million, Kenya had a nominal GDP of just $21 billion and a nominal GNI per capita of $580, ranked 175th in the world. Adjusted for PPP, the GNI per capita was $1,300, or 185th in the world. While the National Rainbow Coalition in 2002 drove the ruling party from power for the first time since independence, the new government's steps to improve economic performance and decrease corruption became entangled in a political conflict over changes to the constitution aimed at curtailing executive power.

History

Home to fossil evidence of some of the oldest known hominid species, Kenya owes most of its modern population to Cushitic speakers migrating from the north in the second millennium BC and Bantu speakers who arrived roughly 2,000 years later. Trade with the Arabian Peninsula and Persian Gulf was under way in the first century AD, and migrants from those regions established port cities along the coast during the Middle Ages.

Portuguese and Omani Control

In 1498, the Portuguese explorer Vasco da Gama visited the main coastal city, Mombasa, on his famous voyage around the Cape of Good Hope to India. Subsequent Portuguese expeditions seized the port and exercised control over the Kenya coast for much of the 16th and 17th centuries. However, beginning in the 1650s, the ruler of Oman sent naval forces to help free the Muslim city-states, and the Portuguese were expelled from Mombasa for the last time in 1729. The coast then enjoyed a high degree of independence under Omani dynasties until the 19th century. The sultan of Muscat, in Oman, began to rule his empire from the island of Zanzibar in present-day Tanzania in 1832, and in 1837 he ousted a rival dynasty from Mombasa to secure control over the whole coastal area. By this time, the small-scale slave trade had expanded significantly, in part to supply labor to new clove plantations on the coastal islands.

Colonization by Great Britain

Great Britain outlawed the slave trade in 1807 and committed itself to suppressing the practice throughout its empire in 1833. The Omani ruler of Zanzibar, a British ally, gradually shut down the slave trade in his domain over the following half century, but other commerce continued to flourish as European, American, and Indian merchants arrived in greater numbers. Christian missionaries and explorers made their way into the interior, and competition between Britain and the newly unified Germany led the two powers to delineate their spheres of influence in East Africa in 1886, in effect drawing the border between modern Kenya and Tanzania. The sultan of Zanzibar transferred his territories on the mainland north of this line to the British East Africa Association the following year, and it received a royal charter as the British East Africa Company in 1888. The British government assumed control from the struggling company in 1895, establishing the East Africa Protectorate.

The British constructed a railroad from Mombasa to Kisumu on Lake Victoria between 1895 and 1901, but their expanding presence met with resistance from local peoples, including the Kikuyu and the Nandi. In the first decades of the 20th century, the British encouraged white settlers to begin large-scale farming in the highlands of the interior. The Kikuyu and other groups were displaced to make way for these settlers and in some cases were confined to reserves. Since the indigenous people had developed no formal land-ownership in the European sense (land was typically held collectively by the tribe or ethnic group), the British legal system confirmed the right of the protectorate to grant title to settlers. After 1920, the territory was divided into the Kenya Protectorate, the coastal area still nominally under Zanzibari sovereignty, and Kenya Colony, encompassing the interior. White settlers were represented in the colony's legislative council.

Kenyans Move Toward Independence

The first indigenous political movement, the Young Kikuyu Association, was organized in 1921 and eventually evolved into the Kenyan African Union (KAU) in 1944. Along with other, similar groups, it sought African representation in the colonial legislature and improved economic and cultural rights for Africans, but its demands were resisted by the colonial government and white settlers. Finally, in 1944, Africans gained limited representation in the legislative council. International and African pressure on Great Britain to decolonize increased after World War II. In 1952, a mainly Kikuyu insurgent group known as the Mau Mau launched a rebellion against colonial rule, and the British declared a state of emergency that lasted until 1960. The rebellion was suppressed in 1956, by which time about 13,000 people had died. Thousands of Kikuyu and other Africans were forcibly relocated by the British as part of their campaign. Jomo Kenyatta, head of the KAU since 1946, was jailed with other nationalist leaders during the state of emergency, accused of orchestrating Mau Mau actions. After the emergency was lifted, a new Kenya African National Union (KANU) was formed, with Kenyatta—released in 1961—as its leader. Africans also won a majority on the legislative council at this time, and negotiations between the British and a coalition headed by Kenyatta resulted in a constitution, elections, and finally independence on December 12, 1963. Kenyatta, the first prime minister, became president when the country converted to a presidential republic under a new constitution in 1964.

The Development of Strongman Rule

Jomo Kenyatta consolidated power by dispensing privileges and economic favors to placate the country's various ethnic groups and by using authoritarian methods to silence critics and potential rivals. Nevertheless, opponents perceived favoritism toward the Kikuyu and suppression of non-Kikuyu leaders. In 1969, an important opposition party was banned and Kenya became a de facto one-party state.

Kenyatta rejected socialism, which was adopted by most other postcolonial independence leaders. He maintained a mostly pro-Western policy orientation as well as the legal features of a capitalist or free market economic system. Instead of nationalizing or seizing the property of settlers, Kenyatta recognized their property rights and arranged an inventive deal with the British government to finance the purchase of white-owned land for redistribution to Africans. Many settlers were thus able to leave the country voluntarily on good terms, while others remained and aided in the country's economic growth. Kenya's initial economic success made it a model for Africa and a target for foreign investment. The economy grew at an average rate of 6 percent from 1971 to 1981, outstripping most other countries on the continent.

Economic and Social Contradictions

Kenyatta's policies represented a contradictory blend of liberalism, corruption, and authoritarianism. While many poor Kenyans received small farms as part of the land redistribution effort, large blocks of land also went to a privileged Kikuyu elite. In one round of government land transfers, 6,070 square kilometers went to a small number of wealthy, mostly Kikuyu owners. Yet Kenyatta also spent a third of the budget on education, and the overall economic growth benefited all Kenyans to some extent, despite expanding wealth disparities.

Economic Freedom

Dictatorship and Economic Deterioration

Kenyatta died in 1978 and was succeeded by his vice president, Daniel arap Moi. Moi ended any ambiguity that remained from Kenyatta's tenure and led Kenya into a more explicit dictatorship. In 1982, the constitution was amended to make the KANU the only legal political party, rendering Kenya a one-party state in law as well as in fact. The judiciary and the press were more tightly controlled by the executive branch, and political repression increased. Corruption spread widely throughout government, with Moi's Kalenjin ethnic group displacing the Kikuyu in prominent positions. Foreign aid and investment subsided as political conditions worsened, and Moi actively sought to limit foreign ownership of industry as part of an Africanization policy. Economic growth rates fell, worsened in part by Kenya's continued vulnerability to drought and the fluctuating world prices of its main agricultural exports, including coffee. But even a booming economy would have been hard-pressed to cope with the country's massive population growth, from about 8 million at independence to the current 37 million. Under these conditions, per capita income dwindled and poverty rates soared.

A Transfer of Power and Democracy Reborn

In 1988, Moi instituted the *mlolongo* (queuing) system of voting, in which voters lined up publicly behind an image of their chosen candidate or party. This denied voters a secret ballot and even the right to abstain. Widespread calls for constitutional reform broke out that year, and the arrest of reform advocates sparked riots. Sensitive to international pressure, Moi agreed to remove the single-party clause from the constitution in 1991.

Facing a divided opposition, Moi easily won multiparty elections in 1992 and 1997, though critics accused him of electoral fraud and other abuses. Furthermore, opposition parties gained 45 percent of the seats in parliament in 1992 and nearly supplanted KANU as the majority in 1997 voting. For the 2002 elections, Moi was constitutionally barred from running for another term, while the opposition had united its various political and ethnic groups into the National Rainbow Coalition (NARC). Opposition politician Mwai Kibaki, a Kikuyu, easily defeated Moi's handpicked candidate, Uhuru Kenyatta, the first president's son but a political novice. NARC routed KANU in the parliamentary elections. It was the first time a peaceful transfer of power had taken place between political parties.

Kenya's Constitution and Democracy

1. (1) All sovereign power belongs to the people of Kenya and shall be exercised only in accordance with this Constitution.

(2) The people may exercise their sovereign power either directly or through their democratically elected representatives.

(3) Sovereign power under this Constitution is delegated to the following State organs, which shall perform their functions in accordance with this Constitution—

(*a*) Parliament and the legislative assemblies in the county governments;

(*b*) the national executive and the executive structures in the county governments; and

(*c*) the Judiciary and independent tribunals.

(4) The sovereign power of the people is exercised at—

(*a*) the national level; and

(*b*) the county level.

2. (1) This Constitution is the supreme law of the Republic and binds all persons and all State organs at both levels of government.

The Constitution of Kenya [Kenya], August 27, 2010. Available at: http://www.unhcr.org/refworld/docid/ 4c8508822.html [accessed 1 February 2013].

President Kibaki initially took serious steps to broaden representation in his government, as well as to decentralize authority, curb corruption, and improve the economy. These policies have led to a return of foreign investment and an increase in economic growth and initiative (see links to two columns by Thomas Friedman in the *New York Times* below). However, two years after Kibaki's election, the government became entangled in controversy over proposed reforms to the constitution. One purpose of the reforms had been to create the position of prime minister and reduce the power of the presidency, but when the final government-backed draft went before voters in a referendum, it contained provisions that actually strengthened the presidency. Opposed by several members of Kibaki's own cabinet, the proposal was rejected by voters, 57 percent to 43 percent. This incident and subsequent actions by Kibaki to consolidate power by favoring his own ethnic group have created political tension ahead of presidential elections scheduled for late 2007. At the same time, the referendum showed that the country had genuinely returned to a democratic path and established a strong sense of political pluralism.

Confronting the Legacy of Dictatorship

Kenyatta and Moi left a difficult economic legacy to overcome. Kenya began its independence as an economic model, only to sink into poverty; it was ranked 152nd on the United Nations Development Programme's 2006 Human Development Index. It confronts these challenges in the midst of the continent's formidable HIV/AIDS crisis, which has taken an enormous human, social, and economic toll. Roughly 1.3 million Kenyans were living with HIV as of 2006, and more than a million children had been orphaned by AIDS. It is now the country's leading killer, ahead of malaria and other infectious diseases, and is rapidly winnowing out the able-bodied population. Life expectancy stands at a mere 47.5 years of age.

Another challenge is rampant corruption. Transparency International has estimated that the average Kenyan must pay 16 bribes per month, most often to police. The judiciary is no less corrupt. Initial steps under President Kibaki to reform the judiciary were promising. According to the Library of Congress Country Profile, "Following the resignation of the chief justice, the anticorruption authority found credible evidence of corruption against five of nine Court of Appeal judges and proof of misconduct against 18 of 36 High Court judges and 82 of 254 magistrates. In October 2003, one-half of Kenya's senior judges were suspended over allegations of corruption, and tribunals were established to investigate the charges against them." Nevertheless, corruption remains a stubborn problem, and government efforts to tackle it have fallen short of expectations. Transparency International gave Kenya a ranking of 150 out of 179 countries in its 2007 Corruption Perceptions Index.

Periodical and Internet Sources Bibliography

The following articles have been selected to supplement the diverse views presented in this chapter.

Jorge Castañeda   "Latin King: How Did a Weakened Chávez Retain Venezuela's Presidency?," *Time*, October 22, 2012.

The Economist   "Cuba: Indecision Time," September 15, 2012.

Tamara Eidelman   "Arrival of Russian Democracy: March 26, 1989," *Russian Life*, March–April 2009.

William W. Finan Jr.   "Stuck with Putin," *Current History*, vol. 111, no. 747, October 2012.

Isabel Hilton   "Desperately Seeking Democracy," *New Statesman*, May 28, 2009.

Paul Johnson   "Vladimir Putin: The World's Most Unlovable Man," *Forbes*, October 22, 2012.

Mac Margolis   "Chávez's Latest Power Grab," *Newsweek*, January 17, 2011.

Berhanu Nega and Geoff Schneider   "Things Fall Apart: Dictatorships, Development, and Democracy in Africa," *Journal of Economic Issues,* vol. 46, no. 2, June 2012.

Michael Petrou   "The End of Democracy?," *Maclean's*, March 3, 2009.

John Restakis   "What Would Che Say About Co-ops?," *New Internationalist*, July/August 2012.

James Sherr   "Putin Is Slipping: The Kremlin's Long-Standing Resident Is Heading for Trouble," *Prospect*, September 19, 2012.

Philip Shishkin   "Watching the Mighty Cockroach Fall," *Newsweek*, February 6, 2011.

What Does the Future Hold for Middle Eastern Governments?

Chapter Preface

Until 2011 the Middle East and North Africa were dominated by dictatorships. Most of the countries in the region had been either formal or informal colonies of the European powers. After World War II, they became independent. Initially, the former colonies were ruled by kings or sultans, but a succession of military coups replaced the monarchies with personal dictatorships. During the Cold War, many of these regimes received economic and military support from the Soviet Union or the United States. Egypt and Tunisia became key allies of the United States in the 1980s. Libya received some support from the Soviets and, in turn, backed anti-Western and anti-Israeli terrorist groups.

The Arab Spring—democratic uprisings throughout the Arab world that began in late 2010—challenged the status quo, ended the reign of a number of dictatorships, and prompted reforms. At various times throughout history, there have been periods of democratic expansion and contraction among dictatorships. Noted political scientist Samuel P. Huntington theorized that there have been three "waves" of democracy. The first started in the late nineteenth century and lasted until World War II. The second wave began at the end of World War II as states such as Germany and Japan began democratic transitions and the period of decolonization commenced. The third wave started in the 1970s and ran through the end of the Cold War as the former Communist states democratized. Some scholars have argued that the events of the Arab Spring are the start of a fourth wave of democratization.

As a result of the Arab Spring, countries such as Egypt, Libya, and Tunisia held democratic elections and created new permanent or interim constitutions. However, the success of Islamist parties in balloting in key states, such as Egypt, led some to question whether the countries were exchanging one form of authoritarianism for another. Critics argued that instead of embracing democracy, these countries were becoming theocracies. While a secular coalition won Libya's July 2012 balloting, Islamist groups were able to win elections in Tunisia and Egypt. Fears emerged that the countries would follow the path of Iran, which in 1979 overthrew longtime dictator Mohammad Reza Shah Pahlavi and replaced the monarchy with a repressive religious government.

The viewpoints in the following chapter examine the impact of the Arab Spring on the region. The authors explore whether a new wave of democracy is spreading through the area or if the entrenched dictatorships will remain in power. The authors also discuss whether the new democracies are regressing back to dictatorships or theocracies, or if they are transitioning into full democracies.

"Libyans in general celebrate . . . the beginning of a new era in their country's political history. They now feel they will set a clock ticking on a plan for a new government."

The Arab Spring Will Lead to the Fall of Dictatorships Across the Middle East

Shankar Kumar

The Arab Spring is a series of uprisings against dictatorial regimes in the Middle East and North Africa that includes the revolution that overthrew Libyan dictator Muammar Gaddafi and started the country down the path toward democracy. According to Shankar Kumar in the following viewpoint, the success of pro-democracy movements in Libya and other countries has led to new rebellions against oppressive governments, including Syria, Bahrain, and Yemen. Kumar is a journalist who writes for the Sahara Times, *an Arab newspaper based in Denmark.*

As you read, consider the following questions:

1. According to the viewpoint, which three countries are under "challenge" from demonstrations and protests?

Shankar Kumar, "International: Dictators at a DISCOUNT," *The Sahara Times*, November 5, 2011. Copyright © 2011 by Athena Information Solutions, Pvt. Ltd. All rights reserved. Reproduced by permission.

2. The Assad family has ruled Syria for how many years?

3. How much money did the "Toyota War" cost Libya, in Kumar's estimation?

Libyans are writing words like "liberated" on Twitter and Facebook to express their happiness following the grisly end of Muammar Gaddafi in Sirte, the last stronghold of the former Libyan dictator. It has had a resonating effect. The whole West Asian and the North African regions are, in fact, gripped by the cataclysmic nature of the event.

Especially in Syria, Yemen and Bahrain, under challenge from public protests, the word "liberated" has gained large attention. A general perception is that anti-regime movement in these countries would get more strident now. Growing public praise in Syria, Yemen and other West Asian nations for Libyan rebels reveals it clearly. Already, Syrians have declared that they will not give a pause to their seven-month-old movement unless they remain successful in ending the dictatorial regime of President Bashar al-Assad, the son of Hafez al-Assad who ruled Syria for 29 years. According to the United Nations, about 3,000 people lost their lives in the President Assad–led crackdown on protesters in the West Asian country since April [2011]. Against this brutal crackdown, international pressure has though mounted on Assad, yet the Syrian president in support of Hezbollah, a militant group with its base in Lebanon, has not stopped his men from shooting down protesters.

Syria and Yemen

Now that Libyans' effort to get their country rid of Gaddafi has fructified, it is felt that opposition forces in Syria may agree to militarise their uprising. Moreover, the Arab League [referring to the League of Arab States] which authorized NATO [North Atlantic Treaty Organization] intervention in Libya, could come under pressure from the Syrian opposition to overthrow the government.

It should be noted that the Assad family has been at the helm of Syrian affairs for more than 41 years. There is nothing like opposition political party there. Only one political party, the Arab Socialist Ba'ath Party led by Bashar al-Assad, has been allowed to hold effective power. Although minor parties are allowed, they are legally required to accept the leadership of the Arab Socialist Ba'ath Party. While this system remained embedded in Syria, Bashar al-Assad introduced minor reform in his country's political and economic structures in 2000. But they were largely cosmetic in nature, and as a consequence simmering frustration remained well entrenched in the hearts of Syrians. Experts say in the age of television and Internet, it is not possible to stop people from remaining uninfluenced by the political developments of other nations. True, it is seen in the case of Yemen too. Taking a cue from successful uprising of Tunisia and Egypt, common Yemenis revolted against President Ali Abdullah Saleh who has been ruling the country since 1978. In June, forces opposed to Saleh fired a rocket into his presidential house compound during a prayer service. The Yemeni president was grievously injured while seven others were killed in this incident.

Since then stringent steps by the Yemeni administration against protesters have led to several deaths, fuelling anger more against President Saleh. In the aftermath of the bloody end of the Libyan dictator, a perception is gaining ground that the Yemeni president could agree to accept asylum from Saudi Arabia rather than risking death at the hands of angry Yemenis. Similarly, the situation is challenging in Bahrain also. Resentment against Prime Minister Salman Al Khalifa is rather brewing stronger with passage of days. Several people have got killed in Bahrain in clashes since the uprising began here in March. Demand is that Prime Minister Salman, who has been ruling the country since 1971, should step down, because he has failed to provide employment and nondiscriminatory

Barack Obama on the Arab Spring

There are times in the course of history when the actions of ordinary citizens spark movements for change because they speak to a longing for freedom that has been building up for years. In America, think of the defiance of those patriots in Boston who refused to pay taxes to a king, or the dignity of Rosa Parks as she sat courageously in her seat [during the civil rights movement]. So it was in Tunisia, as that vendor's act of desperation tapped into the frustration felt throughout the country. [Editor's note: Mohamed Bouazizi committed suicide in public, by setting himself of fire, after police punished him for selling fruit without a license.] Hundreds of protesters took to the streets, then thousands. And in the face of batons and sometimes bullets, they refused to go home—day after day, week after week—until a dictator of more than two decades finally left power.

The story of this revolution, and the ones that followed, should not have come as a surprise. The nations of the Middle East and North Africa won their independence long ago, but in too many places their people did not. In too many countries, power has been concentrated in the hands of a few.

Barack Obama,
"Remarks by the President on the Middle East
and North Africa," White House, May 19, 2011.

treatment to a large section of people in the country. To quell protests, the Bahraini government called troops from Saudi Arabia and UAE [United Arab Emirates], triggering deep hatred towards the Khalifa family. In the background of development in Libya, the raw wounds of Bahrainis, it is feared, may become more intense.

Events in Libya Help Shape the Revolutionary Climate

Still one does not know whether the Western power which jumped headlong in Libya will take similar action in Bahrain, a major base of US naval forces. Nonetheless, the "Arab Spring," as the uprisings in West Asian and North African countries are popularly called, has got a boost from the Libyan development. Already, Twitter has begun to erupt with anti-monarchial writings. While countries like Qatar, UAE and Saudi Arabia supported popular anti-Gaddafi revolt in Libya, their governments are filled with a sense of trepidation that they may too be caught under the whirlwind of pro-democracy revolution.

But then it is in sub-Saharan Africa where Gaddafi was engaged in civil strife and played a role of king of African kings, the word "liberated" has got more consequential meaning. His bloodied demise at the hands of rebels provides obvious answer to it. In fact, Gaddafi used to [be] a destabilizing force in African nations like Cameroon, Chad and Nigeria. The disastrous "Toyota War" of 1986–87 is well known in this regard. Chad, a sub-Saharan country repulsed Tripoli's territorial ambition when the latter attacked the African nation. It led to the killing of 7,000 Libyan soldiers besides costing Gaddafi $1.5 billion. In 1979, he dispatched a contingent to Uganda to help tyrant Idi Amin [Dada] to repulse the Tanzanian invasion. This step proved humiliating for Gaddafi as in the face of onslaught from Tanzania he had to withdraw his army from Kampala.

The Future of Libya

Nonetheless, Libyans in general celebrate the demise of Gaddafi as the beginning of a new era in their country's political history. They now feel they will set a clock ticking on a plan for a new government and constitutional assembly leading to

151

full democracy in 2013. Especially among the youth, the establishment of a democratic government with broad participation is a craze.

They feel that when Gaddafi is dead, all tribes will be united for the cause of the nation. It should be noted that there are more than 140 known tribes in Libya, many of which subdivide into several clans and groups. Apart from Qadhadhfa, a tribe to which Muammar Gaddafi belonged, tribal groups ... have a strong presence in cities like Benghazi and Tripoli, [and] want their pound of flesh in any governing setup formed in the country in the post-Gaddafi period.

Although in the heat of passionate cries for liberation which is presently ringing loud and clear through the streets of Libya, their ego and claim for power are silent, yet many fear the lack of any enemy to unite against could quickly create rifts among them. For the major international players like India, this is a cause of great concern. They fear any kind of discord along tribal lines could delay return of peace and stability in Libya; and this is what the world will not want to happen at a time when the majority of countries are facing economic slowdown. Still the killing of Gaddafi has sent a broad message to the world that dictators can no longer hold on to power amid the call for democracy and good governance.

> "Participatory government and individual rights are 'alien to the Muslim political tradition' because Islam vests authority in God and society must be guided by God's law."

The Arab Spring Will Not Lead to the Fall of Dictatorships Across the Middle East

Laurel E. Miller, Jeffrey Martini, F. Stephen Larrabee, Angel Rabasa, Stephanie Pezard, Julie E. Taylor, Tewodaj Mengistu

In the following viewpoint, Laurel E. Miller and her colleagues argue that the Arab Spring revolts toppled regimes in the Middle East and North Africa, but a variety of challenges and obstacles will make it difficult for the newly freed states of the region to democratize. Instead, the authors assert, the states of the region have employed a variety of tactics that have suppressed democracy and allowed authoritarian leaders to stay in control. Furthermore, some scholars question whether democracy is possible in Islamic countries. The authors are researchers at the RAND Corporation, a libertarian research and public policy think tank.

Laurel E. Miller, Jeffrey Martini, F. Stephen Larrabee, Angel Rabasa, Stephanie Pezard, Julie E. Taylor, Tewodaj Mengistu, *Democratization in the Arab World: Prospects and Lessons from Around the Globe*, Rand, 2012, pp. 35–37, 40–46. Copyright © 2012 by Rand Corporation. All rights reserved. Reproduced by permission.

As you read, consider the following questions:

1. How do the authors identify a hybrid regime?

2. How many countries in the region claimed to be republics prior to the Arab Spring?

3. Are there any specific prohibitions or restrictions on democracy in Muslim tradition or Islamic law, according to the critical view of the Koran's role in government?

The Arab Spring [referring to a series of uprisings against dictatorial regimes in the Middle East and North Africa beginning in late 2010] presents many transformative opportunities for the region, but progress toward democracy remains precarious. Until the recent upending of authoritarian regimes leads to institutionalized democratic practices and real political power is exercised by representative and accountable parliaments, the Arab world will remain the only part of the world that has no consolidated democracies.

Hybrid Regimes

The Arab world has never had a consolidated democracy within its ranks. It does include a few examples of hybrid regimes—ones that have some institutions associated with democracy yet that fall short of popular rule and accountability. In the literature on democratization, these regimes have variously been referred to as competitive authoritarian, electoral authoritarian, and partly free, among other labels. Three hybrid regimes in the Arab world—Lebanon, Kuwait, and Iraq—are often referred to as democratizing regimes, as if their hybrid nature is only a way station on the path to more complete democracy; however, each of these countries faces considerable obstacles to evolving into full-fledged, stable democratic systems.

Authoritarian Regimes

Beyond the Arab world's hybrid regimes, which operate within constitutional systems that have some features of democracy, the region contains a wide variety of more purely authoritarian regimes. Of these, there are seven monarchies—Bahrain, the United Arab Emirates (UAE), Saudi Arabia, Qatar, Morocco, Jordan, and Oman—and, prior to the Arab Spring, there were six republics headed by long-ruling autocrats—Syria, Yemen, Algeria, Libya, Tunisia, and Egypt. Of the republics, as of early 2012, Tunisia was a nascent electoral democracy still in a transitional phase; Egypt had held parliamentary elections but was experiencing a more uncertain transition than Tunisia; and autocratic leaders had been removed in Libya (violently) and Yemen (through negotiation), but transition processes had barely begun.

Monarchies. Saudi Arabia, Bahrain, the UAE, and Qatar have what scholar Michael Herb refers to as "dynastic monarchies," meaning that the family rules, rather than a single individual, and political power is distributed among its members. In most dynastic monarchies, with the exception of Bahrain, succession is decided by family consensus, and a leader can likewise be removed from office if he loses the *bay'a* (allegiance) of his family. In the non-dynastic Arab monarchies—Jordan, Oman, and Morocco—the monarch has absolute power and selects his own successor. In these countries, royal family members may serve in high posts but they do so at the pleasure of the ruler.

Personal rights and citizen political participation vary considerably across the monarchies, but thus far none have mechanisms for holding rulers accountable. For example, in Saudi Arabia citizen participation is limited to elite consultation (*shura*) and elected local councils. Oman has an elected advisory council with no legislative or executive powers. Jordan has open contestation for parliamentary seats and the parliament can override the king's veto with a two-thirds vote, but the king still holds executive authority and appoints the cabinet.

Morocco seems to offer hope that an Arab democracy might one day evolve from an Arab monarchy: In June 2011, King Mohammed VI announced constitutional reforms that appear to transfer some executive authority to the prime minister, who will be selected from the majority party. These changes were very quickly put to a July 2011 referendum in which, after a campaign period dominated by the regime, they were overwhelmingly approved. Because the changes leave the monarch in control of military, security, and religious affairs and because he retains authority to block and create laws by royal decree, the constitutional reform may represent more of a deceptive maneuver, designed to take the air out of protests and bolster the regime's appearance of legitimacy, than a genuine effort to steer the country closer to a parliamentary monarchy.

That said, a degree of political reform has occurred, and Morocco, unlike Egypt and Tunisia, was already classified by Freedom House as "partly free" even before the Arab Spring. Whether the pace of change in Morocco is sufficient to deflect the opposition is an open question, however, particularly if democratization elsewhere in North Africa ratchets up the pressure for change.

Republics. Republican governments in Arab states are difficult to categorize because they tend to be complex hybrids that feature structures associated with personalist, single-party, and military-dominated regimes. As governments evolve, aspects of one regime type may become dominant, but institutional vestiges of other types remain. In the mid-twentieth century, monarchy was the dominant form of government in the Arab world, with most of the "dynasties" having been installed by colonial powers. The move away from monarchy began slowly in the late 1940s but progressed rapidly after 1952, when a group of military officers led by Colonel Gamal Abdel Nasser overthrew Egypt's corrupt and widely despised King Farouk.

As president of Egypt, Nasser led an Arab nationalist movement aimed at discrediting the remaining monarchies and melding the region's states into one United Arab Republic. Nasser and other Arab nationalists declared the monarchies illegitimate because they exclusively served the interests of the ruling families and the colonial powers that established them. They argued that, in contrast, the republics served the interests of the people and protected them against foreign domination. For a region struggling to emerge from foreign control, Arab Nationalism was a powerful ideology and, at the time, self-determination was considered to be a more pressing goal than democratic rule. Therefore, although the new Arab republics in Egypt, Syria, Iraq, Yemen, Algeria, Tunisia, and Libya were authoritarian, at the time of their foundings they were for the most part popular and legitimate.

Most of the republics were founded following coups or anticolonial struggles; consequently, their governments tended to be dominated by military officers. However, over time, the republics, with the exception of Libya, adopted single-party governing structures that varied in terms of the relationship between military and civilian authority. In some republics, such as Algeria and Syria, the civilian governments remain highly dependent on military support. In others, such as Tunisia and Libya, leaders substantially weakened the armed forces in order to reduce the possibility of a coup. Since the 1980s, many Arab republics have started allowing greater electoral competition for national and local offices, though the reforms have had little impact on the ruling parties' dominance of political affairs.

As time passed, Arab republics became increasingly repressive and began to lose their veneer of nationalist legitimacy. Government objectives narrowed and, instead of serving the general public, institutions became means for channeling patronage to loyal regime supporters. In addition, governing control became increasingly concentrated in the hands of individual leaders and support bases contracted. Libya's Muammar Qaddafi established one-man rule soon after coming to power, whereas in other states, such as Egypt and Tunisia, personalist regimes evolved slowly from single-party governments. The extent of autocratic dominance is evidenced by Arab leaders' attempts to have family members succeed them. In Syria, Hafez al-Assad's son Bashar came to power after his death, and, when in office, Libya's former leader Qaddafi, Egypt's former president Hosni Mubarak, and Yemen's former president Ali Abdullah Saleh all maneuvered to have their sons inherit their positions. Before his overthrow, President [Zine El Abidine] Ben Ali in Tunisia was rumored to be grooming his wife Leila to take power upon his demise. With efforts to create self-serving "hereditary republics," patronage, protection, and fear became the main pillars of regime stability, each of which is very costly to maintain. . . .

Cultural Impediments to Democracy

Many political theorists have argued that societies must have certain cultural values for democracy to flourish. Values that these culturalist scholars consider to be prerequisites of democracy include respect for individual responsibility, inclusion, civic participation, and tolerance. Some culturalist scholars add that democracy can only be sustained when the belief that democracy is the most legitimate form of government is widespread among elites and the masses.

When explaining the democracy deficit in the Middle East, scholars who ascribe to this culturalist outlook claim that elements of Muslim or Arab culture run counter to the values required for democracy and, instead, contribute to the entrenchment of authoritarian regimes. According to one strand of this view, participatory government and individual rights

"I have suddenly realised I really like President Assad!," cartoon by Wilf Scott, www .CartoonStock.com. Copyright © by Wilf Scott. Reproduction rights obtainable from www.CartoonStock.com.

are "alien to the Muslim political tradition" because Islam vests authority in God and society must be guided by God's law. As a result, there is no legitimate basis for the sovereignty of man, civil codes, or representative government. Culturalists argue that even though some pious Muslims and Islamist leaders consider democracy an acceptable short-term compromise, their belief in the primacy of God's law will perpetuate their struggle toward their ultimate goal: the creation of a global caliphate that unites religious and political authority.

Critics of this view, however, note that the Koran contains no advice as to what defines Islamic government and that the historic caliphate emerged from a political compromise made to fill the leadership void after the Prophet Muhammad's death. The concept of the caliphate is, they claim, an historical artifact, not a sacred duty that Muslims must fulfill, and there is nothing in Islam's scriptures or traditions that precludes Muslims from being committed democrats.

Another cultural reason proffered for the region's democratic deficit is that Islam fosters a blind acceptance of authority. Beginning in the ninth century, Muslim views of political authority took a "quietist" bent. Fearing civil war and foreign conquest, Muslim scholars argued that believers should not rebel against a leader as long as he proclaims himself a Muslim and can protect society against *fitna* (civil disorder). Other scholars extended the argument, claiming that even an evil ruler was better than anarchy. Although proponents of Islam-centric explanations recognize that the religion's history is filled with groups who justify their fight against tyranny on Islamic grounds, they claim that the "quietist" narrative remains dominant because it continues to be preached by modern *ulama* (Muslim clerics), most of whom are state employees and protect the interests of the region's authoritarian regimes.

Islam and Democracy

When statistically tested, the relationship between Islam and democracy offers mixed results. The economist Robert Barro found that even when standard of living measures were controlled for, there was a pronounced negative relationship between democracy and the percentage of a country's population that is Muslim. Barro wondered if the relationship might be even stronger than the results revealed because he had limited his testing to *direct* effects, whereas religion could *indirectly* affect other variables involving gender inequality and certain measures of standards of living. Steven Fish subjected the inequality thesis to greater scrutiny. He, too, found "strong support for the hypothesis that Muslim countries are demo-cratic underachievers," which he attributed to the subordina-tion of women. In a cross-national study, he found that whether or not a country's population was Muslim, gender in-equality correlated with greater authoritarianism, and that in Muslim countries, authoritarianism was prevalent because in-equality between men and women was stark.

Yet, studies employing different measures or model speci-fications find no relationship between Islam and democracy. Several of these studies claim that Arab countries account for most of the positive relationship between Islam and authori-tarianism. The culturalist explanation for these findings is that the patrimonial tribal origins of modern Arab societies have fostered submission to authority and reduced interest in de-mocratization. Political association mirrors the patriarchal so-cial structures found throughout Arab societies (in families, Sufi orders, clans, and other groupings), promoting absolute submission and the subordination of individual concerns to collective interests. Authors of statistical studies that confirm that Arab states are driving the assumed Islam-authoritarianism connection tend to discount a direct cultural cause, in part because surveys suggest that Arabs are highly supportive of democracy. Instead, they believe that "Arab" must be a proxy for an omitted explanation, such as regional dynamics, internal security funding, colonial experience, or a common regime structure, such as "governments based at least partially on narrow sub-ethnic or tribal allegiances."

> "In fact, even with its post–Arab Spring foreign policy, the U.S. is still engaged in that controversial 'balancing act' with a number of repressive leaders."

America's Unsavory Allies

Uri Friedman

The United States has partnered with many dictators, including Egyptian president Hosni Mubarak and Libya's Muammar Gaddafi. In the following viewpoint, Uri Friedman argues that many oppressive regimes still receive significant military, economic, and diplomatic support from the United States. Although this was true in the George W. Bush administration, it continues to be true during the Barack Obama administration as well. Uri Friedman is associate editor at Foreign Policy.

As you read, consider the following questions:

1. What is the US interest in Uzbekistan, according to the viewpoint?

2. What did Bahrain's Sunni monarchy do during the Arab Spring, according to the author?

Uri Friedman, "America's Unsavory Allies," *Foreign Policy*, October 28, 2011. Copyright © 2011 by The Foreign Policy Group, LLC. All rights reserved. Reproduced by permission.

3. How has the United States given support to Saudi Arabia, according to the viewpoint?

A *A look at some of the bad guys the U.S. still supports.*

The U.S. caught a lot of flak this year for having partnered with Tunisia's Zine el-Abidine Ben Ali, Egypt's Hosni Mubarak, Yemen's Ali Abdullah Saleh, and Libya's Muammar al-Qaddafi before uprisings rocked the Middle East. But in his speech on the Arab Spring in May, President Barack Obama suggested that the days of America narrowly pursuing its interests in the region without the broader priority of promoting reform and democracy were over. "We have embraced the chance to show that America values the dignity of the street vendor in Tunisia more than the raw power of the dictator," Obama declared.

Not entirely. Sometimes, it's difficult to reconcile that revamped formulation of American foreign policy with diplomatic realities. Take two events this week. On Thursday, the *Washington Post* reported that the U.S. is operating a drone base in Ethiopia, a country Freedom House recently downgraded to "Not Free" because of "national elections that were thoroughly tainted by intimidation of opposition supporters and candidates." Only days earlier, Secretary of State Hillary Clinton visited the autocratic central Asian leaders Islam Karimov and Emomali Rakhmon to discuss how they can help with the war in Afghanistan. "If you have no contact you will have no influence, and other countries will fill that vacuum who do not care about human rights," Clinton explained ahead of her visit, adding that "it's a balancing act." In fact, even with its post–Arab Spring foreign policy, the U.S. is still engaged in that controversial "balancing act" with a number of repressive leaders. Let's take a look at eight of the worst offenders.

Teodoro Obiang Nguema Mbasogo

Country: Equatorial Guinea

Record: Since 1979, Obiang has presided over one of the most corrupt countries on Earth. Freedom House notes that he and his inner circle have amassed huge personal fortunes from the country's substantial oil industry while 60 percent of the population lives on less than $1 per day.

U.S. Interest: Salon's Justin Elliott suggests that the Bush administration initially tried to strengthen ties with Equatorial Guinea to secure an alternative to Middle East oil. Under President Bush, exports of Equatorial Guinean oil to the United States increased to 100,000 barrels a day.

U.S. Support: The Bush administration's support of Equatorial Guinea was clear and included several high-level meetings between Obiang and Bush, as well as the reopening of the U.S. Embassy in the Equatorial Guinean capital, Malabo, which had been closed to protest the country's human rights abuses. But it's unclear if President Obama shares the Bush administration's enthusiasm. Sure, Obama did pose for the photo above [not shown] with Obiang, Obiang's wife, and Michelle Obama during a reception at the Metropolitan Museum in New York in September 2009. But, more recently, the Justice Department decided to seize $71 million in allegedly corrupt assets from Obiang's son.

Islam Karimov

Country: Uzbekistan

Record: The former Communist Party leader has ruled Uzbekistan since it gained independence from the Soviet Union in 1991, suppressing all political opposition, winning elections by astronomical margins, and intimidating, fining, and jailing dissidents, independent journalists, and Muslims who worship outside onerous state rules. The most notorious incident under Karimov came in 2005 when security forces fired on a crowd of protesters in the city of Andijan, killing several hundred people, according to rights groups. Stories abound about forced child labor during the cotton harvest and brutal, systematized torture of Karimov's opponents.

U.S. Interest: Republican presidential candidate Herman Cain may pooh-pooh "Ubeki-beki-beki-beki-stan-stan," but the U.S. views Uzbekistan as a critical partner in Afghanistan. As Clinton pointed out during her recent visit to Tashkent, Uzbekistan can help with the war effort by cracking down on al-Qaeda-affiliated Uzbek militants and preventing insurgents from Afghanistan and Pakistan from establishing sanctuaries within its borders. The U.S. also transports non-lethal supplies from Europe to NATO forces in Afghanistan via Uzbek territory. This Northern Distribution Network (NDN) is an attractive alternative to Pakistani supply lines as Washington's relationship with Islamabad sours. "Uzbekistan is the only other country bordering Afghanistan with access to Eurasian railways and a reasonably high-volume rail network," Joshua Foust observes at the *Atlantic*.

U.S. Support: The 2005 Andijan incident poisoned U.S.-Uzbek relations, with the U.S. imposing sanctions and Uzbekistan kicking American troops off its military base there, but the partnership has now blossomed again. In an effort to secure the NDN, the White House is urging a receptive Congress to override a ban on military aid to Uzbekistan linked to the country's poor human rights record (the U.S. already provides Uzbekistan with about $12 million in foreign aid, according to the Center for American Progress). During a visit to a General Motors plant in Tashkent on Saturday, Clinton called the facility a "symbol of our friendship and cooperation" but added that "Uzbekistan needs to continue its reforms in rule of law, democracy, and human rights."

Above [photo not shown], Karimov meets with President Bush at the White House in March 2002.

Hamad Bin Isa Al-Khalifa

Country: Bahrain

US Military Support for the Middle East

Near East	2006 Actual	2007 Actual	2008 Actual	2009 Actual	2010 Estimate	2011 Request
Bahrain	15,593	14,998	3,968	8,000	19,000	19,500
Egypt	1,287,000	1,300,000	1,289,470	1,300,000	1,300,000	1,300,000
Israel	2,257,200	2,340,000	2,380,560	2,550,000	2,775,000	3,000,000
Jordan	207,900	252,900	298,380	335,000	300,000	300,000
Lebanon	3,713	5,020	6,943	159,700	100,000	100,000
Libya					150	250
Morocco	12,375	12,000	3,625	3,655	9,000	9,000
Oman	13,860	13,494	4,712	7,000	11,848	13,000
Tunisia	8,413	8,385	8,345	12,000	15,000	4,900
Yemen	8,415	9,725	3,952	2,800	12,500	35,000
Total Near East	**3,814,469**	**3,911,301**	**4,049,955**	**4,378,155**	**4,542,498**	**4,781,650**

TAKEN FROM: "Foreign Military Financing Account Summary," US Department of State, Washington, DC, June 23, 2010.

Record: Bahrain's Sunni monarchy launched a massive crackdown on mainly Shiite protesters during the Arab Spring with the help of troops from its Sunni allies Saudi Arabia and the United Arab Emirates. According to Human Rights Watch, more than 30 people died in protest-related violence and hundreds more were wounded. While Bahrain lifted its state of emergency in June, the rights group explained in July, "hundreds of those arrested remain in detention and scores have been put on trial in military court."

U.S. Interest: The U.S. Navy has its Fifth Fleet stationed in Bahrain and the Gulf island kingdom is backed by America's staunch ally Saudi Arabia, which serves as a regional counterweight to Shiite-led Iran.

U.S. Support: Shortly before the Arab Spring, Hillary Clinton praised Bahrain for embarking upon a "democratic path." Obama has since called on Bahrain's rulers to implement reforms, but he's held back from speaking out as forcefully against the crackdown as he did with countries like Libya and Syria. The Obama administration is currently delaying a $53 million arms sale to Bahrain until an "independent" Bahraini panel issues a report on alleged human rights abuses during the uprising. Bahrain's foreign minister sat down with *Foreign Policy* yesterday to discuss the standoff.

Above [photo not shown], former Defense Secretary Robert Gates visits Khalifa in Bahrain in December 2008.

Meles Zenawi

Country: Ethiopia

Record: Criticism of Ethiopia currently centers on the 2010 election, when Prime Minister Zenawi's Ethiopian People's Revolutionary Democratic Front won a whopping 99.6 percent of the vote. According to Human Rights Watch, the elections were preceded by "months of intimidation of opposition party supporters" and a government campaign to reserve "access to government services and resources to ruling party members." The rights group adds that while the government released prominent opposition leader Birtukan Midekssa last year, plenty of political prisoners remain in jail.

U.S. Interest: Ethiopia has long been a U.S. ally in the fight against the Islamic militant group and Somali al Qaeda affiliate al-Shabaab, which has carried out attacks across East Africa. This week, we learned that the United States is also operating a drone base in Ethiopia to provide intelligence and coordinate attacks on al-Shabaab in East Africa.

U.S. Support: Back in 2006, the U.S. secretly supported an Ethiopian invasion of Somalia to wipe out an Islamist movement related to al-Shabaab. And while the Obama administration did criticize the 2010 elections, its decision to base a drone program in Ethiopia suggests the alliance is still strong. (Not to mention that the U.S. provides Ethiopia with around $533 million in foreign aid.)

Above [photo not shown], Zenawi (far right) meets with President Bush, former Secretary of State Colin Powell, and former Kenyan President Daniel arap Moi in December 2002.

Emomali Rakhmon

Country: Tajikistan

Record: A 2010 WikiLeaks cable from the U.S. Embassy in Dushanbe discussed the "cronyism and corruption" plaguing central Asia's poorest state, noting that Rakhmon and his family "play hardball to protect their business interests, no matter the cost to the economy writ large." Additionally, in the name of confronting religious fundamentalism in his largely Muslim country, the secular former Soviet apparatchik has cracked down on Muslims wearing veils or beards, banned children under 18 from attending religious services at mosques, demanded that Tajik students studying religion abroad return home, and begun censoring Friday sermons. Rakhmon has also issued many idiosyncratic decrees during his two decades of leadership: In 2007, for example, he announced that he had dropped the Slavic "ov" from the end of his surname and that all babies born to Tajik parents from then on would have to follow suit.

U.S. Interest: Tajikistan, like Uzbekistan, provides the U.S. with a military supply route to Afghanistan.

U.S. Support: During her visit to Dushanbe on Saturday, Clinton emphasized that the U.S. values the "relationship and friendship between our two countries" and is "committed to a long-term partnership." But she also raised concerns about press and religious freedom. In 2010, the U.S. provided Tajikistan with $48 million in foreign aid.

Above [photo not shown], former Defense Secretary Donald Rumsfeld (back to camera) meets with Rakhmon (center) in Dushanbe in July 2005.

Abdullah Bin Abdul Aziz

Country: Saudi Arabia

Record: While King Abdullah may have turned many heads by announcing last month that women would for the first time be allowed to vote, run for local office, and serve on the king's advisory board, Saudi Arabia's human rights record is still pretty abysmal and the country used a show of force— and a lot of money—to quickly silence Arab Spring–inspired protests at home. Human Rights Watch assesses the situation pretty bluntly: "Authorities continue to systematically suppress or fail to protect the rights of nine million Saudi women and girls, eight million foreign workers, and some two million Shia citizens."

U.S. Interest: Saudi Arabia's massive oil wealth and ability to check Iran's power in the region make the kingdom an indispensable U.S. ally.

U.S. Support: One of the most recent examples of America's stalwart support of the regime is a massive $60 billion weapons sale to the Saudis.

Above [photo not shown], King Abdullah presents President Obama with the King Abdul Aziz Order of Merit in Riyadh in June 2009.

Gurbanguly Berdymukhamedov

Country: Turkmenistan

Record: When Berdymukhamedov assumed power in 2006, he initially took steps to dismantle the personality cult surrounding his predecessor, Saparmurat Niyazov or "Turkmenbashi." But Human Rights Watch reports that the government has returned to the "repressive methods of a previous era" by stifling NGOs and Turkmen activists, arbitrarily interfering with people's freedom of movement, obliterating press freedoms, shrouding the prison system in secrecy, and cracking down on followers of more austere forms of Islam.

U.S. Interest: Turkmenistan has opened up its airspace so that the U.S. can transport cargo to Afghanistan. The country is also central Asia's largest gas producer, and Berdymukhamedov discussed energy ties with Hillary Clinton when they met on the sidelines of the U.N. General Assembly in 2009.

U.S. Support: The U.S. provided Turkmenistan with $16 million in foreign aid in 2010. When a reporter asked Assistant Secretary of State Robert Blake, Jr. whether human rights came up in Clinton's 2009 meeting with Berdymukhamedov, Blake reportedly responded that the issue did come up but that in bilateral talks "we've only got a certain amount of time, and so we touch on the most important things. And human rights is not as big an issue in Turkmenistan as it is in some of the other central Asian countries."

Above [photo not shown], Berdymukhamedov waves during a visit to Paris in February 2010.

Truong Tan Sang

Country: Vietnam

Record: The Vietnamese president and senior Politburo member, pictured above [photo not shown] in July 2011, presides over a country that is most often criticized for its crackdown on dissent, which includes Internet censorship and cyber-attacks on dissident websites. Forced labor is a consistent issue as well, Human Rights Watch reports.

U.S. Interest: Vietnam may have once been a bitter foe, but the United States now sees the country as an important ally in Southeast Asia as it seeks to contain China's growing influence in the region and aggressiveness in the South China Sea.

U.S. Support: The U.S. has recently conducted joint naval exercises with Vietnam and struck a deal on nuclear energy through which the U.S. will provide Vietnam with nuclear fuel and technology. The U.S. sends Vietnam about $122 million in foreign aid.

> *"It's important to remember that power-ful Western friends aren't everything. After all, the lesson of Tunisia and Egypt is that dictators sometimes fall despite, not because of, American help."*

Think Again: Dictators

Graeme Robertson

Graeme Robertson tackles a number of myths and misconcep-tions about dictatorships in the following viewpoint. He finds that external support is not enough to prevent dictatorships from falling. However, he also argues that the best way for foreign countries to promote democracy is simply to provide aid and as-sistance to opposition groups in authoritarian regimes and allow them to carry out the struggle to democratize. Robertson is an assistant professor of political science at the University of North Carolina at Chapel Hill and the author of The Politics of Pro-test in Hybrid Regimes: Managing Dissent in Post-Communist Russia.

As you read, consider the following questions:

1. How many countries were listed as not free by Freedom House in 2011?

Graeme Robertson, "Think Again: Dictators," *Foreign Policy*, vol. 186, May/June 2011. Copyright © 2011 by The Foreign Policy Group, LLC. All rights reserved. Reproduced by permission.

2. According to Robertson, did Iran's 2009 Green Revolution succeed?

3. Did the United States support or oppose the dictatorial regime of Chilean general Augusto Pinochet, in the author's view?

*A*rab *autocrats may be tottering, but the world's tyrants aren't quaking in their steel-toed boots.*

"Dictatorships are all about the dictator."

Rarely, if ever. In the first months after the Arab revolutions began, the world's televisions were filled with instantly iconic images of a crumbling old order: the Ben Ali clan's seaside villa on fire in Tunisia, Hosni Mubarak's stilted pre-resignation speeches in Egypt, Muammar al-Qaddafi's rambling, defiant diatribes from a bombed-out house in Libya. They were a reminder that one of the most enduring political archetypes of the 20th century, the ruthless dictator, had persisted into the 21st.

How persistent are they? The U.S. NGO Freedom House this year listed 47 countries as "not free"—and ruled over by a range of authoritarian dictators. Their numbers have certainly fallen from the last century, which brought us quite a list: Stalin, Hitler, Pol Pot, Pinochet, Khomeini, and a host of others now synonymous with murderous, repressive government. But invoking such tyrants, while a useful shorthand in international politics, unfortunately reinforces a troublesome myth: that dictatorships are really only about dictators.

The image of a single omnipotent leader ensconced in a mystery-shrouded Kremlin or a garishly ornate presidential palace took hold during the Cold War. But dictatorships don't just run themselves. Performing the basic tasks expected of even a despotic government—establishing order, levying taxes, controlling borders, and overseeing the economy—requires the cooperation of a whole range of players: businessmen, bureaucrats, leaders of labor unions and political parties, and, of course, specialists in coercion like the military and security forces. And keeping them all happy and working together isn't any easier for a dictator than it is for a democrat.

Different dictatorships have different tools for keeping things running. The Communist regimes of the 20th century relied on mass-membership political parties to maintain discipline, as did some non-Communist autocracies. The authoritarian system that ruled Mexico for 70 years—what Peruvian novelist and Nobel Prize winner Mario Vargas Llosa once called "the perfect dictatorship"—was orchestrated by the nationalist Institutional Revolutionary Party, a massive organization whose influence extended from the president's compound in Los Pinos to the local seats of government in every tiny village. Egypt's recently departed Hosni Mubarak was similarly buttressed for three decades by his National Democratic Party.

Then there's the junta option: a military-run dictatorship. These have advantages—discipline and order, and the capacity to repress opponents, among them—but also drawbacks, most notably a small natural constituency that doesn't extend far beyond the epaulet-wearing classes. The generals who ruled Brazil from 1964 to 1985 solved this problem by offering controlled access to a parliament in which economic elites and other powerful interests could voice their demands and participate in governance. However, this proved to be a difficult balancing act for a military that found it hard to manage elections and the pressures of a public increasingly dissatisfied with its record on the economy and human rights, and the generals ultimately headed back to their barracks.

At the extreme, some authoritarian governments do approximate the dictator-centric regimes of the popular imagination. Mobutu Sese Seko, who ruled Zaire (now the Democratic Republic of the Congo) for more than 30 years, and the Duvalier dynasty in Haiti are classic examples. Here, order is maintained largely by distributing patronage through personal or other networks: clans, ethnic groups, and the like. But paradoxically, these are the most unstable dictatorships. Keeping a government operating smoothly is difficult in the absence of a broad organizational or institutional base, and the whole system rises and falls with the fate of one man.

"The power of the masses can topple autocrats."

Not by itself. In 1989, people power swept across Eastern Europe. Mass strikes in Poland brought the country's Communist rulers to the table to negotiate their way out of power. After hundreds of thousands of people gathered in Prague's Wenceslas Square, one of Eastern Europe's most brutal Communist regimes crumbled and handed over power in Czechoslovakia to a motley crew of playwrights, priests, academics, and friends of Frank Zappa. In East Germany, teeming crowds simply walked out of communism's westernmost showpiece to seek asylum in, and then reunification with, the West. And people power, as Ferdinand Marcos found to his dismay in the Philippines in 1986, was not limited to communism or Eastern Europe.

But there was far more to the collapse of communism in Eastern Europe and autocratic regimes elsewhere than the impressive moral authority of crowds. As the Chinese showed in Tiananmen Square in 1989, capitulating to pro-democracy activists in the streets is hardly the only option. There have been plenty of other places where people power has failed disastrously in the face of a well-organized military response. In Hungary, the popular uprising of 1956 was brutally crushed by Red Army tanks. Burma's 2007 Saffron Revolution produced little more than life sentences for the country's dissident Buddhist monks; Iran's 2009 Green Revolution fell to the batons of the Basij two years later.

What distinguishes people power's successes from its failures? Size, of course, matters, but autocrats tend to fall to crowds only when they have first lost the support of key allies at home or abroad. The Egyptian military's decision to abandon Mubarak and protect the protesters gathered in Cairo's Tahrir Square, for instance, was crucial to the president's downfall this February.

How can demonstrators persuade regime stalwarts to jump ship? In Eastern Europe, the geopolitical sea change engineered by Soviet leader Mikhail Gorbachev and his allies obviously helped—but you can't exactly bring down the Iron Curtain again. Regimes with professionalized militaries separate from civilian authorities might be more vulnerable to defections; regimes based on highly ideological political parties are less likely to see their members break ranks. The credible threat of ending up at the war crimes tribunal in The Hague or having your Swiss bank accounts frozen can work wonders as well. But unfortunately for protesters, predicting authoritarian reactions to uprisings is far from an exact science—which is little consolation when your head is being cracked by a riot cop.

"The more brutal the dictator, the harder to oust."

Unfortunately, true. Reflecting on the French Revolution, Alexis de Tocqueville observed that the "most dangerous moment for a bad government is when it begins to reform." What was correct in the 18th century is, sadly, still true in the 21st. It is probably not a coincidence that the list of authoritarians removed by street protest in recent years is largely populated by rulers whose regimes allowed at least a modicum of political opposition. Tyrants like Serbia's Slobodan Milosevic, Georgia's Eduard Shevardnadze, Kyrgyzstan's Kurmanbek Bakiyev, and Egypt's Hosni Mubarak may have been horrible in many ways, but their regimes were undoubtedly more permissive than those of many who have held onto power to this day.

If this is true, why do any dictators allow opposition in the first place? And why don't they simply go the full Tiananmen at the first sign of protest? Because running a truly ghastly dictatorship is tougher today than it used to be.

The interconnections of 21st-century civilization make it harder to control information and far more difficult and costly to isolate a country from the outside world than it was in the 20th. The death of communism, meanwhile, has robbed leftists and right-wing strongmen alike of a cover story for their anti-democratic practices. In the past decade, rulers of countries such as Uzbekistan and Yemen have used the West's new-found fear of militant Islam—and the logistical necessities of the United States' post-9/11 wars—to similar ends, but they number far fewer than the ideological tyrants who divvied up whole continents under Cold War pretexts a generation ago.

The result is that in more and more places, rulers are compelled to justify their practices by adding a touch of "democracy." Vladimir Putin chose to stand down—though not far down—in 2008 rather than break Russia's constitutional ban against a third consecutive presidential term, and even the Chinese Communist Party allows some competitive elections at the town and village levels. There are exceptions to this trend, of course: Turkmenistan, North Korea, and Burma spring to mind. But such regimes feel increasingly like remnants of the late, unlamented 20th century, rather than harbingers of things to come.

"Personality cults are crazy."

Crazy like a fox. Do North Koreans really believe that Kim Jong-il can change the weather based on his mood? Do Libyans think Qaddafi's *Green Book* is a brilliant work of political philosophy? Do Turkmen really think that the Ruhnama, the religious text authored by their late post-Soviet dictator—and self-styled spiritual leader—Saparmurat Niyazov, is a sacred scripture on par with the Quran and the Bible?

The US Response to the Arab Spring

Foreign assistance will be a key element of our response to the Arab Spring [referring to a series of uprisings against dictatorial regimes in the Middle East and North Africa beginning in late 2010]. But I think it's important to emphasize that we are devoting to this cause all our tools of statecraft: the daily diplomacy we undertake with governments; increased outreach to civil society, to new political actors, and to the youth activists who are driving events on the ground; trade and investment; and the work we undertake together with others in the international community to ensure that, as these countries move down the path of democratic change, they find a warm welcome and a helping hand from the global community of democracies.

Tamara Wittes,
"Can Foreign Assistance Bolster the Arab Spring?,"
US Department of State, July 21, 2011.

Probably not, but for the dictators' purposes, they don't have to. As political scientist Xavier Márquez has argued, personality cults are as strategic as they are narcissistic. Part of the problem that dictators' would-be opponents face is figuring out who else opposes the leader; compelling the populace to publicly embrace preposterous myths makes that harder still. Official mythmaking is also a means of enforcing discipline within the regime. Stalin—the progenitor of the modern dictator personality cult—understood well that his self-mythologizing would be too much for some of his old comrades to swallow; Lenin, after all, had specifically warned against it. But those who might have objected were swiftly dispatched. For the apparatchiks who remained, submitting to the cult was humiliating—and humiliation is a powerful tool for controlling potential rivals.

But personality cults, like most authoritarian technologies, have their drawbacks. The bigger the cult, the bigger the challenge of succession. Heirs to the throne really have just two options: dismantle the cult or go one better. The former is perilous; in the Soviet Union, Nikita Khrushchev's famous 1956 secret speech—the posthumous critique of Stalin that gave us the term "personality cult"—was, after all, secret, deemed too explosive for the Soviet public. Today, North Korea's ruling Kim family illustrates the hazards of the alternative: Now that the official newspapers have already reported that the current Dear Leader, Kim Jong-il, has mastered teleportation, what's his son and newly designated heir, Kim Jong-un, supposed to do for an encore?

"Sometimes it takes a dictator to get the job done."

Actually it doesn't. The past two years have not done much to advertise the abilities of the Western democratic model of government to take large and painful but necessary actions. Frustrated over everything from a failure to balance budgets to an apparent inability to face up to the challenges of climate change, more than a few Westerners have turned their gaze wistfully toward the heavy-handed rule of the Communist Party in China. "One-party autocracy certainly has its drawbacks," the *New York Times*' Thomas Friedman wrote in a 2009 column. "But when it is led by a reasonably enlightened group of people, as China is today, it can also have great advantages." This March, Martin Wolf wrote in the *Financial Times* about how "China has achieved greatness."

This romanticizing of authoritarianism is not new; Augusto Pinochet's murderous regime in 1970s Chile was once cheered by many in Washington as an ugly but necessary instrument of economic reform. Yearning for a strong hand, however, is rooted in several fallacies. First, it conflates the failings of one form of democracy—in Friedman's case, the gridlocked American version—with an entire category of governance. Second, it assumes that dictators are more able than democrats to undertake unpopular but essential reforms. But unpopular decisions don't simply become popular because an autocrat is making them—just remember the late North Korean finance chief Pak Nam-gi, who ended up in front of a firing squad following the public backlash against the confiscatory currency reform the Kim regime pushed through in 2009. In fact, authoritarians, lacking the legitimacy of popular election, may be even more fearful of upsetting the apple cart than democrats are. In Putin's Russia, for instance, leaders are unable to dial back the massive military expenditures that keep key constituencies quiet but that even their own ministers recognize to be unsustainable.

Besides, suggesting that dictators can force better policies upon their people assumes that a dictator is likely to know what those better policies are. The idea that there are technocratic solutions to most economic, social, and environmental problems might be comforting, but it is usually wrong. Such questions rarely have purely technical, apolitical answers—and only in a democracy can they be aired and answered in a way that, if not entirely fair, is at least broadly acceptable.

"Digital revolutions are bad news for autocrats."

Not necessarily. New technologies—from the fax machine to the Internet to Facebook—have invariably been heralded as forces for upending dictatorial regimes. And of course, if cell phones and Twitter made no difference at all, then pro-democracy activists wouldn't use them. But the real test of technology is its ability to shift the balance of power between dictators and those trying to unseat them—to make revolutions more frequent, faster, or more successful. And though it's too early to know for sure, the arc of revolutions in 2011 doesn't look that different so far from the lower-tech upheavals of 1989, or, for that matter, 1848.

What makes a difference is how quickly authoritarians can work out how to counter a new innovation, or use it themselves. Sometimes this happens quickly: The barricades invented in Paris that made the revolutions of 1848 possible were briefly useful, but militaries soon figured out how to use cannons against them. Similarly, today's authoritarians are already learning how to use cell phones and Facebook to identify and track their opponents. In Iran, for instance, Facebook posts, tweets, and emails were used as evidence against protesters in the wake of the failed Green Revolution.

As it happens, some of the most enduring innovations have been the least technological. Mass protests, petitions, and general strikes, though now ubiquitous tactics, were at first ideas as novel as Twitter, and they have continued to play a crucial role in spreading democracy and civil rights around the world. It's a useful reminder that not all the new tools that matter come in a box or over a Wi-Fi connection.

"Dictatorship is on the way out."

Not in our lifetime. The recent upheavals in the Middle East, though inspiring, have happened against a gloomy backdrop. Freedom House reported that in 2010, for the fifth year in a row, countries with improving political and civil rights were outnumbered by ones where they were getting worse—the longest such run since the organization started collecting data in 1972. Two decades after the Soviet Union's collapse, democracy may be robust in formerly Communist central Europe, Latin America, and even the Balkans, but most former Soviet states remain quite authoritarian. And though a few Arab countries are newly freed of their tyrants, they are still very much in transition. Being poor or corrupt, as Egypt and Tunisia are, does not rule out being democratic—think of India— but it does make it harder to build a stable democratic system.

Nevertheless, the Arab revolutions have offered a spark of hope, one that has clearly worried dictators in places as far off as Moscow and Beijing. The question is what the world's liberal democracies should do, or not do, to push things along. Survey the United States' long history of democracy-promotion successes and failures, and the inescapable lesson, even setting aside recent adventures in Iraq and Afghanistan, is that less is usually more. Providing aid—as the United States did to the opposition in places like Serbia, Ukraine, and Georgia—or simply setting an example are better means of toppling a dictator than actually doing the toppling.

But in either case, it's important to remember that powerful Western friends aren't everything. After all, the lesson of Tunisia and Egypt is that dictators sometimes fall despite, not because of, American help.

> *"Democracy . . . is a rather novel introduction to our part of the world. . . . Our ancestors lived in the realm of god-kings where ruler and the state was one and the same thing."*

After the Dictators

Sholto Byrnes

In the following viewpoint, Sholto Byrnes argues that East Asia provides a good framework to understand the complexities of the democratic transitions of the Arab Spring. Byrnes examines the rise of democracy in states such as Indonesia and Singapore and explores the lessons those examples have for Middle Eastern countries such as Egypt and Tunisia. He concludes by asserting that the road to democracy is long and arduous and that democracy does not look the same for all peoples and all cultures. Byrnes is a journalist and contributing editor for the New Statesman.

As you read, consider the following questions:

1. The People Power Revolution of 1986 ended the rule of which dictator, according to Byrnes?

Sholto Byrnes, "After the Dictators," *New Statesman*, September 12, 2011, pp. 30, 32–33. Copyright © 2011 by New Statesman. All rights reserved. Reproduced by permission.

2. How many people does Byrnes estimate were killed in Hama in 1982 when Syrian dictator Hafez al-Assad suppressed the Muslim Brotherhood?

3. What was Indonesia's inflation rate in 1966, according to the author?

*W**ant to know what will happen in the Arab world after the fall of despots such as Gaddafi and Mubarak? The place to look is Asia.*

After weeks of riots, demonstrations and bloody counter-attacks, the dictator at last stood down. His promised reforms were not enough. Eventually the armed forces, from whose ranks he had emerged and whose loyalty had shored up his regime for nearly 30 years, would no longer support him. Some feared that when elections were held, Islamists would take over. In the event, the first fair presidential vote did bring to power the leader of a Muslim organisation; but moderation prevailed. The country's citizens were too attached to their newly won freedom to allow anyone to restrict their rights again.

A decade on, corruption is rife, many of the dictator's past associates are big political players, and the former ruler was never brought to account for the human rights violations that took place on his watch. But change has come. The US president has hailed the country as a model for how Muslim-majority autocracies can become pluralist democracies.

This is an outline of what happened when a long-serving dictator fell from power in 1998—General Suharto of Indonesia. Can something similar happen in the Middle East and North Africa? For decades of their post-independence history, the countries of the Far East and Southeast Asia were ruled by autocrats. One by one, however, nearly all the despots have fallen, or stepped down, or begun to open up their state's political sphere and relinquish power. In some countries, the change happened dramatically, as in Indonesia and in the

Philippines' People Power Revolution of 1986, which saw off Ferdinand Marcos. In others, "soft authoritarians" such as Singapore's Lee Kuan Yew and Malaysia's Mahathir Mohamad voluntarily terminated long periods in office. Democracy today may be limited, as it is in Singapore, shaky (Cambodia) or intermittent (Thailand). But principles of good governance, such as independence of the judiciary, took root so quickly in South Korea and Taiwan that both countries have tried and convicted democratically elected presidents.

Throughout the region, repression is on the wane. The cheers for democracy have been unstoppable. So, what lessons can East Asia offer to an Arab world awakening to a new revolt in which the despotic leaders of Egypt, Libya, Tunisia and, in effect, Yemen have departed while others, notably in Syria and Bahrain, sweat in their gilt-edged beds?

To borrow a phrase from the *Jakarta Globe* columnist Karim Raslan, "an authoritarian consensus" existed in both regions: economic development was the trade-off for lack of democracy and civil rights. The leaders of these lands used the same tool—varying forms of anti-colonial rhetoric—and not just those who had won their position through revolution or armed struggle, as in the case of Egypt's Gamal Abdel Nasser and Indonesia's Sukarno, but also monarchs such as Norodom Sihanouk of Cambodia, whom the French had placed on the throne thinking he was a playboy they could manipulate, but who ended up touring the world demanding his country's independence.

In both regions, stability was a prize attained only with great effort—the boundaries of many countries had been drawn by the colonial powers, and frequently created artificial barriers between ethnic groups or lumped together historically antagonistic peoples. That prize was palpably fragile, but the consequent imperatives of "national unity" also became a convenient excuse for heavy-handed police action, risible elections and the restriction of liberties. This was overlooked by the West, however, for the dictators were our allies.

In the implicit bargain between autocratic leaders and their populaces, everything hung on the prospect of prosperity. In his 2007 modern social history *Asian Godfathers: Money and Power in Hong Kong and Southeast Asia*, Joe Studwell argued that the countries he covered had enjoyed a "developmental honeymoon". In this state, he wrote:

> Populations are unusually willing to trust authority and their leaders' promises to deliver continuous improvements in standards of living. When south-east Asians were told that free association of labour was antithetical to growth . . . and that constraints on individual freedom and the media are part of Asian culture, they acquiesced.

When the honeymoon soured or came to an abrupt end, the regimes fell. It was not anger about human rights abuses that brought Suharto down, but his government's catastrophic response to the Asian financial crisis of 1997. Eleven years earlier, if an ailing President Marcos had not lost control of the Philippines' economy, his wife, Imelda, might have been able to carry on expanding her notorious shoe collection.

People can tolerate plutocratic elites so long as some of the wealth appears to trickle down. For most of the time, it did in East Asia. Not so, or not sufficiently, in West Asia and its environs. And it is not just in this that the Arab dictators have worse records than their Western-backed East Asian predecessors. In terms of targeted massacres of their own people, for instance, few of them went as far as promising the "rivers of blood" that Colonel Gaddafi wanted rebellious Libyans to suffer. Nor could many match Syria's destruction of the town of Hama in 1982, when up to 40,000 people died in President Hafez al-Assad's attempt to wipe out the Muslim Brotherhood in his country. A desire for punitive retribution is understandable. But, judging by the precedents in East Asia, it should be resisted.

This is because if there is one thing that has marked the transition towards democracy in East Asia, it has been an almost bewilderingly magnanimous accommodation with the past. In Indonesia, several of Suharto's top generals have been on the ticket in presidential elections; one, Susilo Bambang Yudhoyono, is the incumbent. Marcos's widow is in the Philippines congress, and their son is a senator. Cambodia's prime minister, Hun Sen, is a former member of the Khmer Rouge and was also premier of the Vietnamese-installed People's Republic of Kampuchea in the 1980s. Pol Pot's genocidal regime fell over 30 years ago, but only five senior Khmer Rouge cadres have faced trial so far, and one has been convicted. There appears to be little appetite for the UN-backed war crimes court to bring more to justice.

Strategic Amnesia

Occasionally, the willingness to ignore the dictators' past atrocities and embrace their memory is quite incomprehensible to the outside world. In the Philippines, there have been calls for Marcos to be honoured with a state funeral. And last year the Indonesian government proposed to make Suharto a "national hero". The award-winning author Tash Aw, whose first two novels are set in Malaysia and Indonesia, puts it thus: "I think it is a typically Asian way of dealing with the trauma of history: we have to ignore the ugly truth of what happened in the past in order to move forward."

This amnesia can also be explained partly by a necessity to salvage something from the strongmen's decades. If the dictators and autocrats were entirely bad, even evil, then swaths of the years these states have been independent must be regarded as shameful. Indonesia, for instance, was ruled from 1945 to 1998 by two such men—Sukarno and then Suharto. Can its people only celebrate the last 13 years of its existence? Moreover, at the time they took power, these men nearly all drew on local sources of legitimacy and enjoyed tremendous popu-

"Democracy ... one man one vote ... I'm a man and I've got the one vote what's the problem?," cartoon by Lindsay Foyle, www.CartoonStock.com. Copyright © by Lindsay Foyle. Reproduction rights obtainable from www.CartoonStock.com.

larity. Many were involved in the liberation struggle. Quite a few were elected to begin with, as were Marcos, Sukarno and Sihanouk (when he renounced the throne to become prime minister in 1955), while those parliamentary autocrats, Mahathir and Lee Kuan Yew, earned their leadership time and again in national polls. Even Ne Win, who led the military coup in Burma in 1962 and ruled until 1988, had become prime minister entirely legally in 1958, and duly handed power back after 17 months.

Neither are their records as unequivocal as Western observers usually portray them. They were mostly successful at maintaining stability—dictators tend to be good at that—but also in bringing millions out of poverty. In a region where Lee Kuan Yew could proudly title the second volume of his memoirs *From Third World to First*, raising standards of living was an achievement neither ignored at the time nor forgotten today. Western-style pluralistic liberal democracy was absent from Hong Kong, Singapore, South Korea and Taiwan in the 1970s and 1980s; but that was also when their astonishing growth led them to become known as the Asian Tiger economies. All his crimes cannot take away from Suharto that he reduced Indonesia's inflation rate from 650 per cent in 1966 to under 20 per cent within three years; and his harshest critics will admit that substantial progress was made in education, health care and infrastructure.

It is not that the populations of these countries are not aware that, in many cases, "these people stole their money, and with relative impunity", says Bridget Welsh, an associate professor at Johns Hopkins and Singapore Management universities. "But there comes a point when these individuals become part of the national story. Their legacy is in things that people can identify with, like roads and schools."

Similarly in the Middle East, the revolutions that brought the generation of Pan-Arab nationalist leaders to power were "popular" in both the political and the quotidian senses, at least initially. The memory of the most prominent of those men, Gamal Abdel Nasser, remains sufficiently inspiring that, in the early days of the Arab Spring, Al Jazeera reported images of the former Egyptian president being "raised in Cairo and across Arab capitals by people who were not even alive when Nasser died in 1970". He was a dictator nevertheless, as was his successor-but-one, Hosni Mubarak. Will the latter be remembered only for his tyranny? Or will future generations of Egyptians recall the air force commander who became a hero of the 1973 Yom Kippur War? The Gulf monarchs, on the other hand, have not only kept their part of the economic bargain (easy, with all that oil) but are the heads of ruling families that for generations have stood at the apex of tribal hierarchies.

If an emphasis on reconciliation rather than truth is a feature of the post-dictator landscape, then so is a rather different form of democracy from the kind practised in the West. It will almost certainly be one in which religion assumes a prominence that would dismay secularists. It is also likely to be one in which a very different notion of liberty prevails. "You place so much value on individuals' rights that you forget that the majority has rights also," Malaysia's Mahathir told me in an interview last year. He, and other proponents of the "Asian values" theory, reject Western-style liberal democracy on the grounds that it is based on foreign social, cultural, religious, ethnic and economic factors, and that it constitutes a "reckless free-for-all".

As the highly respected Singapore-based political scientist Farish A. Noor wrote recently: "Democracy, it has to be remembered, is a rather novel introduction to our part of the world. Prior to that, our ancestors lived in the realm of god-kings where the ruler and the state was one and the same thing. Our real concern should be whether the peoples of the Arab world ... know how to handle the public domain with the care it deserves. This includes having to learn the rules of participatory democracy while on the go."

We should certainly lend whatever help we can to countries newly embracing such challenges. Beyond that, however, the lessons from East Asia's transitions towards democracy are for the outside world to refrain from judging too loudly when dynastic tendencies emerge; from lecturing when our standards of transparency and governance are not met; and above all from intervening and taking control of the process. The US and other Western countries, Welsh says, "have to recognise that they can't do it themselves. Invasions and no-fly zones put them, and not the people who need to be, in the driving seat. Telling people that things need to be done for them just infantilises them."

It took the nations of the West hundreds of years to make the same journey. We should not be too quick to criticise if others stumble on a path that is new to them—or choose to go a different way.

Periodical and Internet Sources Bibliography

The following articles have been selected to supplement the diverse views presented in this chapter.

Elliott Abrams	"Dictators Go, Monarchs Stay," *Commentary*, October 2012.
John Barry and Christopher Dickey	"The Dictator Protection Plan," *Newsweek*, February 20, 2011.
Steve Coll	"Days of Rage," *New Yorker*, October 1, 2012.
David Cortright	"Gandhi on the Nile: Civil Resistance in the Middle East," *Commonweal*, March 11, 2011.
Martin Fletcher	"Gaddafi's Ghost," *Prospect*, June 20, 2012.
Robert Kagan	"To the Shores of Tripoli," *Weekly Standard*, September 5, 2011.
Nicolas Pelham	"A War of Bees That Sting," *New Statesman*, September 26, 2011.
Michael Petrou	"One Giant Leap for Democracy in Egypt," *Maclean's*, May 23, 2012.
Aarti Ramachandran	"Inside the Authoritarian State: Islam and Technology: Evolution and Revolution," *Journal of International Affairs*, vol. 65, no. 1, Fall/Winter 2011.
Amin Saikal	"Authoritarianism, Revolution and Democracy: Egypt and Beyond," *Australian Journal of International Affairs*, vol. 65, no. 5, November 2011.
Jonathan Spyer	"Inside Free Syria," *Weekly Standard*, February 27, 2012.
Jonathan Steele	"A Way Out of Syria's Catastrophe," *Nation*, October 15, 2012.

For Further Discussion

Chapter 1

1. Robert D. Kaplan argues that dictatorships can enact positive changes for people. Does he make a persuasive case that dictators have been beneficial to some societies in Asia? What are the main characteristics that set Asia apart from other areas of the world, according to Kaplan?

2. According to the viewpoint by Sergiu Vidican, dictators share some common traits. What are these similarities? Are there instances when democratic leaders also share some of these traits? Explain.

3. Sishuwa Sishuwa contends that dictator Muammar Gaddafi actually improved the lives of the Libyan people. According to Sishuwa, what were Gaddafi's main accomplishments? Would a democratically elected leader have been able to achieve the same results? Explain.

Chapter 2

1. Pauline H. Baker asserts that Myanmar has begun to democratize. What steps toward democratization have occurred? Is there still a danger that the country will revert to dictatorship?

2. According to the viewpoint by John Fraser, North Korea is likely to remain a dictatorship even if the current regime falls from power. Does the author make a good argument? What are the main weaknesses in the viewpoint?

3. Joseph Contreras contends that Cuba's youth are more likely to demand changes to the island's dictatorial government than are older generations. Why do young Cubans seek change? What are the chances they will succeed in prompting the government to reform?

Chapter 3

1. In her viewpoint, Alice O'Keeffe explores the ways in which Venezuelan leader Hugo Chávez has undermined democracy in Venezuela. What does O'Keeffe assert has been the greatest danger from Chávez's actions? Could Venezuelan society heal itself under a different leader?

2. Jerome Y. Bachelard and Richard R. Marcus are highly critical of Madagascar's 2009 coup. What were the main reasons that the coup plotters cited for the overthrow of the previous government? Did any of their arguments have merit?

Chapter 4

1. Shankar Kumar writes that the fall of the dictatorship in Libya accelerated efforts to get rid of dictators in other countries in the region. What are the main obstacles or challenges that pro-democracy advocates face in countries such as Bahrain? Are they likely to overcome those challenges?

2. In his viewpoint, Sholto Byrnes argues that East Asia provides a good framework to understand the ramifications of the uprisings taking place in the Middle East and North Africa. What examples does Byrnes provide to support his argument? Do you agree with his argument? Explain.

Organizations to Contact

The editors have compiled the following list of organizations concerned with the issues debated in this book. The descriptions are derived from materials provided by the organizations. All have publications or information available for interested readers. The list was compiled on the date of publication of the present volume; the information provided here may change. Be aware that many organizations take several weeks or longer to respond to inquiries, so allow as much time as possible.

Brookings Institution
1775 Massachusetts Avenue NW, Washington, DC   20036
(202) 797-6000 • fax: (202) 536-3623
e-mail: communications@brookings.edu
website: www.brookings.edu

Formed in 1927, the Brookings Institution is one of the most preeminent and well-respected nonprofit, nonpartisan research centers in the United States. The organization sponsors research on democracy, economic and social welfare, and international relations. The Brookings Institution annually publishes a number of research monographs and reports on national and international issues.

Carnegie Endowment for International Peace
1779 Massachusetts Avenue NW, Washington, DC   20036
(202) 483-7600 • fax: (202) 483-1840
e-mail: info@ceip.org
website: www.carnegieendowment.org

The Carnegie Endowment for International Peace was founded in 1910 to promote peace and stability in the international system. The independent, nonprofit research group is headquartered in Washington, DC, but also has offices in Moscow, Beijing, Beirut, and Brussels. The organization supports international efforts to promote peace and democracy. It issues a range of influential publications, including the well-known international relations journal *Foreign Policy*.

Cato Institute

1000 Massachusetts Avenue NW, Washington, DC   20001
(202) 842-0200 • fax: (202) 842-3490
e-mail: pr@cato.org
website: www.cato.org

The Cato Institute was founded in 1977 to promote libertarianism. The institute is a nonprofit organization that opposes tyranny and dictatorships through its promotion of limited government, the free market, and individual choice. Cato conducts seminars, meetings, and public forums each year, and its scholars provide public commentary on a range of issues. The organization also publishes books, studies, and issue reports.

Center for International Policy

1717 Massachusetts Avenue NW, Suite 801
Washington, DC   20036
(202) 232-3317 • fax: (202) 232-3440
e-mail: cip@ciponline.org
website: www.ciponline.org

The Center for International Policy (CIP) is a nonprofit, left-of-center organization founded in 1975. Headquartered in Washington, DC, CIP supports efforts to increase transparency in foreign policy and to promote democracy, demilitarization, and human rights. CIP was critical of US support for right-wing dictatorships in Latin America in the 1980s and has recently argued for an end to economic sanctions on Cuba.

Center for Strategic and International Studies (CSIS)

1800 K Street NW, Washington, DC   20006
(202) 887-0200 • fax: (202) 775-3199
e-mail: aschwartz@csis.org
website: http://csis.org

The nonprofit, nonpartisan Center for Strategic and International Studies (CSIS) was founded in 1962 at Georgetown University to craft innovative solutions to international problems. With more than two hundred scholars and staff members, CSIS is one of the world's largest policy think tanks. CSIS analyzes both US domestic and foreign policy. The center publishes studies and reports on all areas of global politics, including the leading journal the *Washington Quarterly*.

Council on Foreign Relations (CFR)

1777 F Street NW, Washington, DC   20006
(202) 509-8400 • fax: (202) 509-8490
e-mail: pdorff@cfr.org
website: www.cfr.org

The Council on Foreign Relations (CFR) was formed in 1921. It is a nonpartisan, nonprofit research organization with offices in New York and Washington, DC. The CFR seeks to provide resources for its members, policy makers, and the business community as they address the leading international issues of the day. The CFR produces a wide range of publications, including the journal *Foreign Affairs*, which often includes essays by leading politicians from around the world.

Freedom House

1301 Connecticut Avenue NW, Floor 6
Washington, DC   20036
(202) 296-5101 • fax: (202) 293-2840
e-mail: info@freedomhouse.org
website: www.freedomhouse.org

Freedom House was founded in 1941 to promote freedom and human rights around the world. The organization has two main offices, one in New York and one in Washington, DC. Freedom House promotes governance through training, analyses, and support for democratic groups. It also provides reports and studies on democratic governance and individual freedom. Every year Freedom House issues an annual freedom index that ranks countries around the world in categories such as overall freedom, freedom of the press, and freedom of the Internet.

Hoover Institution

434 Galvez Mall, Stanford University
Stanford, CA   94305-6010
(650) 723-1754
e-mail: schieron@stanford.edu
website: www.hoover.org

The Hoover Institution was founded at Stanford University in 1919 by future US president Herbert Hoover. It is a conservative think tank with offices at Stanford University and in Washington, DC. The institution is active in studying both domestic policy and international relations. It publishes a number of academic journals, including the *Hoover Digest* and *Policy Review*, as well as books through the Hoover Institution Press.

International Institute for Strategic Studies

Arundel House, 13–15 Arundel Street, Temple Place
London   WC2R 3DX
44 (0) 20 7379 7676 • fax: 44 (0) 20 7836 3108
website: www.iiss.org

The International Institute for Strategic Studies (IISS) is a nonprofit British institute devoted to the study of international relations and global security. Founded in 1958, the IISS initially focused on nuclear deterrence. Currently it addresses a full range of economic, political, and security issues throughout the world, including many studies regarding the impact of democracy on the international system. It has more than twenty-five hundred members in more than one hundred countries. IISS publishes the highly influential research series the *Adelphi Papers*.

National Endowment for Democracy (NED)

1025 F Street NW, Suite 800, Washington, DC   20004
(202) 378-9700
e-mail: info@ned.org
website: www.ned.org

The National Endowment for Democracy (NED) is a private, nonprofit grant-making foundation dedicated to the growth and strengthening of democratic institutions around the world. It was founded in 1983 and has been actively involved with democratic struggles all over the world, serving as a hub for resources. The organization provides access to research and analysis of democratic development around the world.

Reporters Without Borders
Southern Railway Building, Fifteenth & K Street NW
Suite 600, Washington, DC   20005
(202) 256-5613
e-mail: dcdesk@rsf.org
website: http://en.rsf.org/

Reporters Without Borders was formed in France in 1985 to combat press censorship and to assist journalists in danger around the world. The organization has affiliated correspondents in 150 countries, and it works with local reporters and governments to minimize restrictions on the media, including electronic media. Reporters Without Borders also publishes an annual ranking of countries, based on freedom of the press.

Bibliography of Books

Harlan Abrahams and Arturo Lopez-Levy — *Raúl Castro and the New Cuba: A Close-Up View of Change.* Jefferson, NC: McFarland & Co., 2011.

Daron Acemoglu and James A. Robinson — *Economic Origins of Dictatorship and Democracy.* New York: Cambridge University Press, 2006.

Fouad Ajami — *The Syrian Rebellion.* Stanford, CA: Hoover Institution Press, 2012.

Christopher Alexander — *Tunisia: Stability and Reform in the Modern Maghreb.* New York: Routledge, 2010.

Thomas Ambrosio — *Authoritarian Backlash: Russian Resistance to Democratization in the Former Soviet Union.* Burlington, VT: Ashgate, 2009.

William Avilés — *Global Capitalism, Democracy, and Civil-Military Relations in Colombia.* Albany: State University of New York Press, 2006.

Randall Baker, ed. — *Transitions from Authoritarianism: The Role of the Bureaucracy.* Westport, CT: Praeger, 2002.

Vernon Bogdanor — *The Monarchy and the Constitution.* Oxford, England: Clarendon Press, 1995.

Michael Breen — *Kim Jong-il: North Korea's Dear Leader.* Hoboken, NJ: Wiley, 2012.

Jason Brownlee · *Authoritarianism in an Age of Democratization.* New York: Cambridge University Press, 2007.

Valeria Bunce, Michael McFaul, and Kathryn Stoner-Weiss, eds. · *Democracy and Authoritarianism in the Post-Communist World.* New York: Cambridge University Press, 2010.

Barry Cannon · *Hugo Chávez and the Bolivian Revolution: Populism and Democracy in a Globalised Age.* New York: Palgrave Macmillan, 2009.

Sonia Cardenas · *Human Rights in Latin America: A Politics of Terror and Hope.* Philadelphia: University of Pennsylvania Press, 2010.

Thomas Carothers · *Confronting the Weakest Link: Aiding Political Parties in New Democracies.* Washington, DC: Carnegie Endowment for International Peace, 2006.

Thomas Carothers and Marina Ottaway, eds. · *Uncharted Journey: Promoting Democracy in the Middle East.* Washington, DC: Carnegie Endowment for International Peace, 2005.

Amy Chua · *World on Fire: How Exporting Free Market Democracy Breeds Ethnic Hatred and Global Instability.* New York: Anchor Books, 2004.

Erik A. Claessen   *Stalemate: An Anatomy of Conflicts Between Democracies, Islamists, and Muslim Autocrats.* Santa Barbara, CA: Praeger, 2010.

John F. Clark   *The Failure of Democracy in the Republic of Congo.* Boulder, CO: Lynne Rienner Publishers, 2008.

Nonie Darwish   *The Devil We Don't Know: The Dark Side of Revolutions in the Middle East.* Hoboken, NJ: Wiley, 2012.

Christian Davenport   *State Repression and the Domestic Democratic Peace.* New York: Cambridge University Press, 2007.

Larry Diamond, Marc F. Plattner and Daniel Brumberg, eds.   *Islam and Democracy in the Middle East.* Baltimore, MD: John Hopkins University Press, 2003.

Robert Elgie and Sophia Moestrup, eds.   *Semi-Presidentialism Outside Europe.* New York: Routledge, 2007.

Natasha M. Ezrow and Erica Frantz   *Dictators and Dictatorships: Understanding Authoritarian Regimes and Their Leaders.* New York: Continuum Books, 2011.

Lloyd C. Gardner   *The Road to Tahrir Square: Egypt and the United States from the Rise of Nasser to the Fall of Mubarak.* New York: New Press, 2011.

Richard Gillespie and Richard Youngs, eds.	*The European Union and Democracy Promotion: The Case of North Africa.* Portland, OR: Frank Cass Publishers, 2002.
Marshall I. Goldman	*Petrostate: Putin, Power, and the New Russia.* New York: Oxford University Press, 2008.
Robert E. Goodin	*Reflective Democracy.* New York: Oxford University Press, 2003.
Clement M. Henry and Robert Springborg	*Globalization and the Politics of Development in the Middle East.* New York: Cambridge University Press, 2010.
Ariel Heryanto and Sumit K. Mandal, eds.	*Challenging Authoritarianism in Southeast Asia: Comparing Indonesia and Malaysia.* New York: RoutledgeCurzon, 2003.
Lindsey Hilsum	*Sandstorm: Libya in the Time of Revolution.* New York: Penguin Press, 2012.
Ian Jeffries	*Contemporary North Korea: A Guide to Economic and Political Developments.* New York: Routledge, 2010.
Ashraf Khalil	*Liberation Square: Inside the Egyptian Revolution and the Rebirth of a Nation.* New York: St. Martin's Press, 2012.

Suk Hi Kim, Terence Roehrig, and Bernhard Seliger, eds. — *The Survival of North Korea: Essays on Strategy, Economics and International Relations*. Jefferson, NC: McFarland & Co., 2011.

Stephen J. King — *The New Authoritarianism in the Middle East and North Africa*. Bloomington, IN: Indiana University Press, 2009.

Todd Landman — *Protecting Human Rights: A Comparative Study*. Washington, DC: Georgetown University Press, 2005.

Steven Levitsky and Lucan A. Way — *Competitive Authoritarianism: Hybrid Regimes After the Cold War*. New York: Cambridge University Press, 2010.

Ilja A. Luciak — *Gender and Democracy in Cuba*. Gainesville, FL: University Press of Florida, 2007.

Hans Maier, ed. — *Totalitarianism and Political Religions: Concepts for the Comparison of Dictatorships: Theory and History of Interpretation*. New York: Routledge, 2007.

Lee Marsden — *Lessons from Russia: Clinton and US Democracy Promotion*. Aldershot, UK: Ashgate, 2005.

Paul McCaffrey, ed. — *The Arab Spring*. Ipswich, MA: H.W. Wilson, 2012.

Sarah E. Mendelson and John K. Glenn, eds.

The Power and Limits of NGOs: A Critical Look at Building Democracy in Eastern Europe and Eurasia. New York: Columbia University Press, 2002.

Josephine Syokau Mwanzia and Robert Craig Strathdee

Participatory Development in Kenya. Burlington, VT: Ashgate, 2010.

Erik Paul

Obstacles to Democratization in Southeast Asia: A Study of the Nation-State, Regional and Global Order. New York: Palgrave Macmillan, 2010.

Victor V. Ramraj and Aran K. Thiruvengadam, eds.

Emergency Powers in Asia: Exploring the Limits of Legality. New York: Cambridge University Press, 2010.

Lex Rieffel, ed.

Myanmar/Burma: Inside Challenges, Outside Interests. Washington, DC: Brookings Institution Press, 2010.

David F. Schmitz

The United States and Right-Wing Dictatorships, 1965–1989. New York: Cambridge University Press, 2006.

Gene Sharp

From Dictatorship to Democracy: A Conceptual Framework for Liberation. New York: New Press, 2012.

Dina Shehata

Islamists and Secularists in Egypt: Opposition, Conflict, and Cooperation. New York: Routledge, 2010.

Joshua Stacher   *Adaptable Autocrats: Regime Power in Egypt and Syria.* Stanford, CA: Stanford University Press, 2012.

Milan W. Svolik   *The Politics of Authoritarian Rule.* New York: Cambridge University Press, 2012.

Charles Tilly   *Contention and Democracy in Europe: 1650–2000.* New York: Cambridge University Press, 2004.

William J. Topich and Keith A. Leitich   *The History of Myanmar.* Santa Barbara, CA: Greenwood, 2013.

Klaus von Beyme   *Parliamentary Democracy: Democratization, Destabilization, Reconsolidation, 1789–1999.* New York: St. Martin's Press, 2000.

Leonard Weinberg, ed.   *Democratic Responses to Terrorism.* New York: Routledge, 2008.

Laurence Whitehead, ed.   *Emerging Market Democracies: East Asia and Latin America.* Baltimore, MD: John Hopkins University Press, 2002.

Wissam S. Yafi   *Inevitable Democracy in the Arab World: New Realities in an Ancient Land.* New York: Palgrave Macmillan, 2012.

Fareed Zakaria   *The Future of Freedom: Illiberal Democracy at Home and Abroad.* New York: W.W. Norton & Co., 2007.

Index

D

CPSIA information can be obtained
at www.ICGtesting.com
Printed in the USA
FFOW031909290513
1231FF

9 780737 763157